Windows to Language, Literacy, and Culture

Insights From an English-Language Learner

Cynthia H. Brock

University of Nevada, Reno

Reno, Nevada, USA

Taffy E. Raphael

University of Illinois at Chicago

Chicago, Illinois, USA

800 Barksdale Road, PO Box 8139
Newark, Delaware 19714-8139, USA
www.reading.org

The International Reading Association attempts, through its publications, to provide a forum for a wide spectrum of opinions on reading. This policy permits divergent viewpoints without implying the endorsement of the Association.

Director of Publications   Dan Mangan
Editorial Director, Books and Special Projects   Teresa Curto
Managing Editor, Books   Shannon T. Fortner
Acquisitions and Developmental Editor   Corinne M. Mooney
Associate Editor   Charlene M. Nichols
Associate Editor   Elizabeth C. Hunt
Production Editor   Amy Messick
Books and Inventory Assistant   Rebecca A. Zell
Permissions Editor   Janet S. Parrack
Assistant Permissions Editor   Tyanna L. Collins
Production Department Manager   Iona Muscella
Supervisor, Electronic Publishing   Anette Schütz
Senior Electronic Publishing Specialist   R. Lynn Harrison
Electronic Publishing Specialist   Lisa M. Kochel
Proofreader   Stacey Lynn Sharp

Project Editor   Elizabeth C. Hunt

Cover   Design, Linda Steere; Photo, Comstock

Library of Congress Cataloging-in-Publication Data

Brock, Cynthia H.

  Windows to language, literacy, and culture : insights from an English-language learner / Cynthia H. Brock, Taffy E. Raphael.

       p. cm. -- (Kids InSight)

  Includes bibliographical references (p.   ) and index.

  ISBN 0-87207-580-X

  1. English language--Study and teaching--Foreign speakers. 2. English language--Study and teaching--United States. 3. Language and culture--United States. 4. Literacy--United States. I. Raphael, Taffy. II. Title. III. Series.

  PE1128.A2B687 2005

  428'.0071--dc22

2005016604

For Deng

Contents

Note From the Series Editor   vii

Kids InSight Review Board   x

Acknowledgments   xii

Chapter 1
Setting the Context: Working With Deng   1

Chapter 2
Developing a Knowledge Base About
Language and Culture   15

Chapter 3
Whole-Group Instruction: Unique Challenges
for English-Language Learners   33

Chapter 4
Small-Group Instruction: Applications
to Deng's Learning   52

Chapter 5
Evaluating and Reflecting
on Deng's Learning   67

Chapter 6

Book Club *Plus*: An Alternative Framework   79
for Working With English-Language Learners

References   104

Index   110

Note From the Series Editor

It is a pleasure to introduce readers to Cynthia Brock, Taffy Raphael, Deng Moua, and the students and teachers in a fifth-grade and a fourth-grade classroom in *Windows to Language, Literacy, and Culture: Insights From an English-Language Learner*. Deng, the focal student in the book, is a Hmong English-language learner (ELL) from Laos. In *Windows to Language, Literacy, and Culture*, Cynthia and Taffy help us understand the cultural and historical backgrounds of students like Deng and how students' cultural experiences have an impact on their literacy learning. They also carefully describe Deng's literacy learning and what it was like for Deng to learn to be literate as he participated in various activities in Mrs. Weber's classroom. Adding to the power of the book's message is the unique research approach that undergirds the study. Cynthia and Taffy asked Deng to review and interpret videotapes of literacy lessons over the school year and comment on events and interactions, and the insights from this process are compelling. I am pleased to see that this important, research-based report was selected by a respected panel of literacy experts to be published in the Kids InSight (KI) series; I believe that the book makes an outstanding contribution to the field of literacy.

The KI series provides practical information for K–12 teachers and brings to the fore the voices of and stories about children and adolescents as the basis for instructional decisions. Books in the series are designed to encourage educators to address the challenge of meeting the literacy needs of all students as individuals and learners in and out of our classrooms, while recognizing that there are no easy answers or quick fixes for achieving this goal. Sociocultural perspectives of how students learn are the foundation of each KI book, and authors address learners' emotional, affective, and cognitive development. Strategies and actions embraced by teachers described in KI books include the following:

- dialoguing with other professionals;
- reading research findings in literacy and education;
- inquiring into teaching and learning processes;
- observing, talking with, and listening to students;
- documenting successful practices; and
- reflecting on literacy events using writing and analysis.

Authors of these books allow us to see into classrooms or view students' lives outside of school and learn about the thoughts and dreams of young people as well as the goals and planning processes of teachers. Finally, we are privy to how events actually unfold during formal and informal lessons—the successful and the less-than-successful moments—through the use of transcripts and interview comments woven throughout KI books.

As we read *Windows to Language, Literacy, and Culture*, Cynthia and Taffy show us how to keep kids *in sight* as they describe Deng's literacy learning in whole-class and small-group settings and how the interaction patterns in these various contexts support, or do not support, ELL students' learning. The authors describe how for the first time in several years, Deng spent his entire day in a mainstream fifth-grade classroom with no language support. He had to work hard to learn English and the content necessary to be successful in school. Cynthia and Taffy make a case that supportive, knowledgeable, and caring teachers are needed to work with students like Deng to ensure successful learning. We also see the level of scaffolding and empathic listening necessary for ELL students' learning.

Cynthia, Taffy, Deng, Mrs. Weber, and the students in Mrs. Weber's classroom also help us glean insights as we examine what they do to address tensions that arise during literacy lessons. We see how complex and challenging teaching ELLs can be. A good example described by the authors is during a whole-group reading lesson in which Mrs. Weber seeks to help her students understand a passage from the book *Maniac Magee* (Spinelli, 1990). The concept the teacher is seeking to unpack is the way most people place individuals into categories by skin color and assign stereotypical attributes to each category. In the passage under discussion, the main character, Maniac, does not see people in categories of black or white with respect to skin color. Rather, he sees people as individuals, and he values the variety of interesting skin tones and perspectives they bring to the world. In the middle of the lesson, Mrs. Weber asks the students to stand up, form a semicircle, and extend their arms so they can examine each other's skin tones and see the subtle varieties of colors. Deng participates in the activity, but, as we later learn, he does not understand the directions or the tool of analogy that Mrs. Weber uses to help students understand the concept in the story. As we continue to read *Windows to Language, Literacy, and Culture* and the discussions between Cynthia and Deng, we see a recurring pattern: Deng often did not understand the text he was asked to read, the characters' motives or thoughts, or the events because his understanding was predicated on an understanding of the culture in which the story was situated. As teachers, we learn about these types of issues by listening in on the stimulated recall sessions between Cynthia and Deng as they watch videotapes of various lessons.

In chapter 6 we step back from Deng's experiences in Mrs. Weber's classroom to visit Ms. Trost's fourth-grade classroom in Chicago, Illinois, USA. Ms. Trost works with ELLs and supports their learning using different instructional contexts and interaction patterns. Ms. Trost's ELL students benefit from the way she has organized literacy instruction; helpful lessons can be learned from examining her classroom lesson transcripts.

Throughout *Windows to Language, Literacy, and Culture*, Cynthia and Taffy help readers grapple with complex teaching and learning issues by allowing us to look closely at classroom events and listen to interactions between teachers and students. Through the Reflection Points in each chapter, the authors urge us to write responses to questions posed, gather data from our own classrooms, reflect upon what we see, and generate new possibilities for what could be. There is much to be learned about how to support the learning of ELL students like Deng. Carefully crafted case studies, like the one detailed in this Kids InSight book, will support teachers as they work toward this goal.

Deborah R. Dillon
Series Editor
University of Minnesota, Twin Cities
Minneapolis, Minnesota, USA

Kids InSight Review Board

Jan Turbill
University of Wollongong
Wollongong, New South Wales,
   Australia

Angela Ward
University of Saskatchewan
Saskatoon, Saskatchewan, Canada

Deborah A. Wooten
University of Tennessee
Knoxville, Tennessee, USA

Josephine P. Young
Arizona State University
Tempe, Arizona, USA

Acknowledgments

We are grateful to many people for their support, encouragement, and input throughout the process of writing this book. Susan Florio-Ruane and Jim Gavelek shaped significantly the ideas that framed the design and implementation of the study on which this book is based. Many friends—including classroom teachers, English as a second language (ESL) teachers, district-level administrators, and university teachers and researchers—provided invaluable feedback on earlier drafts of this work. In particular, we thank Rachael Anderson, Kelley Clare, Judy Wallis, Robert Rueda, and the members of WIRED research/writing group to which Cindy belongs at the University of Nevada, Reno. Elisabeth Trost, the outstanding teacher featured in the last chapter of this book and a founding member of the Book Club for English Language Learners Study Group in Chicago, shared with us her invaluable insights about working with English-language learners. We appreciate the opportunity to work with and learn from Elisabeth and the children in her classroom and to learn from the other members of the Book Club for English Language Learners Study Group in Chicago. Deborah Dillon, the series editor for the Kids InSight series, has provided invaluable support, guidance, and encouragement throughout the entire process of writing this book. Elizabeth Hunt at the International Reading Association expertly guided us through the publication process.

We extend special thanks to Deng, Vue, and Mrs. Weber for their participation in the research project on which this book is based. Deng and his family accepted us into their home and allowed us to study Deng's literacy learning with him. This work was much richer because of

Vue's invaluable contributions as a mediator in conversations with Deng and his family. Mrs. Weber and her students graciously opened their classroom to us and invited us to explore Deng's learning there. Finally, we wish to thank the Spencer Foundation for its financial support to engage in the research on which this book is based and for seeing value in studying Deng's literacy learning opportunities.

Chapter 1

Setting the Context:
Working With Deng

Assuming that you are a classroom teacher reading this book, we begin with a question for you: Have you ever taught English-language learners (ELLs) in your classroom? If not, chances are good that you will teach these students at some point in your career. According to Thomas and Collier (2001), ELLs will make up 40% of the school-age population in U.S. schools by the 2030s. The reason educators need to attend to this population of children is that they are currently underserved in U.S. schools (Thomas & Collier, 2001).

In this book, we look closely at the actual classroom literacy learning experiences of an ELL—a Hmong child named Deng (pseudonym)—who immigrated with his family to the United States from Laos via Thailand. Our examination with Deng of his learning will not serve as a single sample of the learning of a child from a different culture that can be generalized to all ELLs in all contexts. Instead, our in-depth conversations with Deng can reveal to you insights about him and his classroom context that can inform your own thinking about your work with ELLs in your unique context. Eisner (1998) suggests that "every particular is also a sample of a larger class. In this sense, what has been learned about a particular can have relevance for the class to which it belongs" (p. 103). Thus, this in-depth look at Deng's literacy learning may raise your consciousness about features in your own context that merit your consideration as you work with ELLs.

Working with Deng, we examined his literacy learning opportunities in his fifth-grade classroom, where English was the medium of instruction. We sought to understand what it was like being a student participating in Deng's classroom literacy lessons from his perspective as an ELL and an insider to his classroom community. To that end, we asked Deng to work with us to offer his interpretations of different literacy events in which he participated.

One of the ways we studied Deng's learning with him was to view videotaped literacy lessons from his fifth-grade classroom with him at his home along with a Hmong–English interpreter named Vue. Vue was a senior in a local high school and always present when Deng watched and interpreted his literacy lessons. Vue and his family also had emigrated from Laos via Thailand, and Vue had lived in the United States for eight years before working with us as an interpreter. Because Deng was in the process of learning English, we felt that an interpreter was necessary so that Deng could make comments and pose questions in either Hmong or English. During the viewing sessions, Deng controlled the television remote and stopped the videotaped lessons in which he had participated whenever he wished to make comments, ask questions, or express confusion about some aspect of the lessons. One evening after Deng, Vue, and Cindy (the first author of this book) had viewed several lessons, Deng handed Cindy a Valentine's Day gift—a booklet of coupons—that he had made at school (see Figure 1). On each page he listed the various things for which Cindy could redeem coupons. For example, one coupon was for Cindy to help Deng with his homework for an hour. (Cindy tutored Deng weekly to help Deng with his schoolwork.) Another coupon was good for Deng watching and commenting in an hourlong videotaped lesson pertaining to the children's book *Maniac Magee* (Spinelli, 1990). Deng's Valentine's Day gift to Cindy reflected the various ways that she worked with him, and it revealed his interest in helping Cindy and Taffy (the second author of this book) explore his learning with him.

The Importance of Listening to Children

As educators, we have long recognized the value of listening to and learning from students. For example, a unique feature of *The Book Club*

Figure 1
Deng's Valentine's Day Gift to Cindy

This book of Valentine Coupons is
presented with LOVE to

Cindy Brock

A coupon may be redeemed, anytime, by
presenting it to

Deng

This Valentine Coupon is good
for one

Watching unit of
maniac magee.

This offer, made with love,

by *Deng*

Connection: Literacy Learning and Classroom Talk (McMahon & Raphael, 1997) was a chapter written—with Cindy's assistance—by three elementary schoolchildren who had experienced Book Club, a literacy curriculum in which small, student-led groups read, write about, and discuss a common book. The chapter offered the students' perspectives about, understandings of, and advice about Book Club for a teacher audience. We subsequently wrote an article (Brock & Raphael, 2003) about our learning as we worked with, and learned from, the students across the two-year process of writing the book chapter. More than a decade ago, we began to explore together the literacy learning of a child from Vietnam, Mei (pseudonym), as she engaged in Book Club (e.g., Brock & Raphael, 1994; Goatley, Brock, & Raphael, 1995; Raphael & Brock, 1993). An important focus of these studies was to take a close and careful look at the ways in which Mei experienced literacy instruction in her mainstream classroom. One central goal was to attend carefully to Mei's evolving thinking and understandings in the context of her literacy lessons.

Our interest in working with students from diverse cultural and linguistic backgrounds, as well as our work with many preservice and inservice teachers of students from diverse backgrounds, reflects several broader national trends. There are large and growing numbers of students in the United States who do not speak English as their first language and whose cultural backgrounds vary (August & Hakuta, 1997; Garcia, 1990; Schecter & Cummins, 2003). According to Walker-Moffat (1995), during the 1980s the United States experienced the greatest influx of immigrants since the beginning of the 20th century. By the late 1980s, more than 75% of all students enrolled in the United States' 15 largest school systems were from culturally and linguistically diverse backgrounds (The National Coalition of Advocates for Students [NCAS], 1988, as cited in Cummins, 1994). Between 1990 and 2000, in some states the population of ELLs in U.S. schools (pre-K–12) more than doubled (National Clearinghouse for English Language Acquisition & Language Instruction Educational Programs, 2002).

While the student demographics in U.S. schools are changing dramatically, however, the teaching force is not. Almost 90% of teachers in the United States are European American, monolingual women from lower middle to middle class backgrounds (Freeman & Freeman, 2002).

Reflection Point 1.1 _____

Keep track of your thoughts and ideas in a journal as you read this book. At this point, stop reading momentarily to collect your thoughts about why a mismatch between the languages and cultures of U.S. students and their teachers might be important. This issue is central to this text.

_____

Mismatches between teachers' and students' cultural and linguistic backgrounds matter because such mismatches *can* impact negatively students' opportunities for academic success in school (Howard, 1999; Nieto, 1999). The important news, however, is that teachers with the necessary knowledge base and positive dispositions toward diversity can provide powerful and meaningful contexts for all the students in their classrooms to be successful (Frank, 1999; Major & Brock, 2003). For example, Ladson-Billings (1994) studied both African American and European American teachers who supported—very successfully—the learning of African American students in their classrooms. Debbie Diller (2003), a European American elementary schoolteacher from a midwestern U.S. community, documented her own professional growth as she learned to change her teaching practices to meet the needs of the African American students in her urban classroom.

The effective teachers described by Ladson-Billings and Diller, and other teachers who successfully teach students whose backgrounds differ from their own, have several characteristics in common. First, they understand that good teaching is not transcendent. That is, good teaching "is a contextual and situational process. As such, it is most effective when ecological factors, such as prior experiences, community settings, cultural backgrounds, and ethnic identities of teachers and students, are included in its implementation" (Gay, 2000, p. 21). Second, they understand that, as humans, we all have personal histories and cultural backgrounds that shape the ways we view the world and act on and within it (Eisner, 1998). For us, as educators, this means that we must develop an awareness that teaching practices in the United States, in general,

---

Box 1.1
Resources on Listening to Students

Hudson-Ross, S., Miller Cleary, L., & Casey, M. (1993). *Children's voices: Children talk about literacy*. Portsmouth, NH: Heinemann.

Kotlowitz, A. (1991). *There are no children here: The story of two boys growing up in the other America*. New York: Anchor Books.

Michie, G. (1999). *Holler if you hear me: The education of a teacher and his students*. New York: Teachers College Press.

Schultz, K. (2003). *Listening: A framework for teaching across differences*. New York: Teachers College Press.

Taylor, D. (1993). *From the child's point of view*. Portsmouth, NH: Heinemann.

---

are based on European American cultural norms and values (Gay, 2000). These norms and values can vary significantly from the cultural norms and values of the many students in our classrooms who have different cultural backgrounds. Thus, when we work with students whose backgrounds are different from ours, there is much we can learn about language and culture to aid us in our work with them. Finally, effective teachers of students from diverse backgrounds understand that the students themselves can provide invaluable insights into their thinking, learning, and lives that we, as educators, can draw from as we design instruction for them. (See Box 1.1 for resources on listening to students.)

In fact, scholars such as Erickson and Shultz (1992) and Pearson (1997) argue that students' perceptions of their learning experiences have largely been neglected in the educational literature. By listening carefully to students themselves, and by couching our learning from Deng and other ELLs in the broader conversations of other scholars and educators in the field, we seek to explore more effective ways to meet the literacy learning needs of all students in our classrooms.

The Collaborators

Taffy and Cindy met Deng in the mid-1990s at Oakland Elementary School, located in a midsize midwestern U.S. community. Our respective paths to this point of convergence were literally continents and cultures apart. The following describes how we came to work together, our backgrounds, and more in-depth information about Deng, who is the center of this story.

Cindy

Cindy was born in Washington state and grew up in rural central Oregon. After earning a bachelor's degree in elementary education, with an emphasis in mathematics, at Oregon State University in 1981, she began teaching sixth grade in a small community south of Portland, Oregon. In this initial teaching position, Cindy first began teaching students from different countries and cultures, in particular, a small number of immigrants from southeast Asia. Cindy had several students from Cambodia and Vietnam in her sixth-grade classroom during her second and third years of teaching. It was fortunate that these students had acquired some proficiency in English prior to moving to Oregon and enrolling in Cindy's classroom because none of her university course work had prepared her to work with students from other countries who did not speak English. Further, at that time, her district had no English as a second language (ESL) teachers or professional development pertaining to ESL.

After three years as a sixth-grade teacher in Oregon, Cindy enrolled full time in a master's degree program in reading and language arts at Washington State University. She chose this major because she felt that her undergraduate preparation in mathematics—while important—had left her with many questions about how to teach reading and writing. After earning her degree, Cindy spent the next six years teaching at the upper elementary level. Her teaching experiences with the Los Angeles Unified School District in California, the School Board of Palm Beach County in Florida, and the Waverly School District in Lansing, Michigan, gave her a much broader exposure to students and families from cultural and linguistic backgrounds different than her own.

In 1991, Cindy began work on a doctorate in educational psychology, with an emphasis in literacy, at Michigan State University. Taffy became Cindy's graduate advisor and invited her to work on various research projects with Taffy and her colleagues. Taffy and Cindy began working on the first of a series of studies about how ELLs experience literacy instruction, specifically using the literature-based instructional framework Book Club (McMahon & Raphael, 1997). Central to this study was Mei, the young literacy learner from Vietnam.

During the mid-1990s, Taffy and Cindy worked with three elementary schoolteachers on assessment related to literature-based instruction. One of the teachers, Mrs. Weber, was a fifth-grade teacher at Oakland Elementary School in Michigan. Because of Cindy's interest in exploring, in depth, the literacy learning of an ELL, Mrs. Weber agreed to allow Cindy to work in her classroom. Deng, one of the students in this classroom, was the ELL with the least proficiency in the class. Deng's mother gave Cindy permission to explore his literacy learning with him, and Taffy provided guidance throughout the two-year study of Deng's literacy learning.

Taffy

Taffy was born in Chicago, Illinois, and grew up in a small industrial town approximately 20 miles south of the city. She earned her teaching credentials as an undergraduate at Michigan State University and then taught fourth grade in a Chicago suburb for a year before moving to Winston-Salem, North Carolina, where she taught intermediate grades during the first year in which schools began court-ordered desegregation through school busing programs. While teaching in two high-poverty settings, first in an inner-city elementary school and then in a rural elementary school, Taffy became interested in issues of equity. In particular, during the first few years of her teaching she saw how unequal early school preparation affected the intermediate students with whom she worked, and how the formation of reading groups led to de facto forms of segregation. She was concerned about how to teach reading so that students who were seriously behind in their abilities would experience more than a year's growth in a year's time, which would give them a chance to catch up with their more privileged peers. That led to Taffy's work toward her master's degree in reading at the University of North Carolina at Greensboro, and from there to a doctoral degree. Taffy began her doctoral studies at the University of Minnesota, before moving to the Center for the Study of Reading at the University of Illinois at Urbana-Champaign to focus on reading comprehension instruction.

Taffy was a professor at Michigan State University when Cindy entered the doctoral program. She had been working with a team of educators to create and research Book Club. In the elementary school where most of the Book Club research was taking place at the time, there were few ELLs, and those few participated in pull-out programs designed to immerse them in English. The Book Club teachers, typical of most teachers, were not sure how best to support those few ELLs during Book Club. Mei, one of the ELLs in the initial Book Club studies, helped Taffy begin to appreciate some of the complexities of providing needed support and to raise questions about what could be done to provide such support within the Book Club framework. It was during that time that Taffy and Cindy met and began to work together on this question.

Deng

Deng Moua and his family came to the United States in 1994, and Taffy and Cindy met Deng in Mrs. Weber's classroom at Oakland Elementary in 1995. After meeting Deng, Taffy and Cindy questioned why he and his family had left Laos to come to the United States. As a result of interviews with Deng's mother (with a Hmong–English interpreter), wide reading about the recent history of the Hmong people, and Cindy's travels to Laos and Thailand to interview a host of individuals associated with the Hmong in those countries, Taffy and Cindy learned that Deng and his family's journey to Michigan was a part of the broader social, cultural, and historical context of many Hmong in southeast Asia. Thus, in order to understand the Moua family's personal journey to the United States and the complex cultural and linguistic background Deng brought to his U.S. classroom, it is necessary to explore the recent history of the Hmong in southeast Asia and the United States. A host of economic, political, and social factors caused many Hmong, like the Moua family, to leave Laos for Thailand and resettle in developed countries such as the United States. We touch on but a few pertinent issues here that shed light on some of the Moua family's possible reasons for leaving their homeland.

The Hmong originated in southwest China, but many left in the 1800s because of intense persecution there and fled to Burma, Laos, Vietnam, and Thailand, with the largest concentration of Hmong fleeing to the mountainous regions of northern Laos (Chan, 1994). Laos had more than 60 different ethnic groups, and the Hmong—one of the minority groups—tended to remain fairly isolated from most majority and other ethnic groups (Walker-Moffat, 1995). In the mountain regions where they lived, the Hmong typically engaged in slash-and-burn agriculture to grow two primary crops: rice and poppies (interview with F. Edmonton, diplomat with the American Embassy, Vientienne, Laos, January 19, 1996; all names of individuals with whom Cindy spoke in southeast Asia are pseudonyms).

During the Vietnam War, the lives of most Hmong in Laos were forever changed when they became involved with the U.S. government. The U.S. Central Intelligence Agency (CIA) enlisted the help of many Hmong—led by the Hmong General Vang Pao—in a "Secret War" to fight against the Communists in North Vietnam and to attempt to prevent a Communist takeover in Laos (Hamilton-Merritt, 1993). The CIA was not successful on either count. When the U.S. troops left Laos, and the Communists gained control, those Hmong who sided with the United States during the war suffered persecution, torture, and death at the hands of the new Communist government in Laos. Many Hmong fled Laos for refugee camps in Thailand. Others remained in the hills of their mountainous homelands to continue fighting soldiers in the new Communist regime.

One of the questions Cindy asked various officials in Thailand and Laos in January 1996 was why Hmong people, such as the Moua family, continued to leave Laos for Thailand as late as the late 1980s and why many Hmong people continued to be resettled from refugee camps in Thailand to developed nations until the 1990s, even though the Vietnam War had ended 20 years before. We discuss some of the complex reasons that Hmong people's lives were still being affected seriously by the aftermath of the Vietnam War.

Many Hmong did not want to leave their homeland in Laos, so some attempted to stay and survive. But, because of continuous danger from the still-Communist government in Laos, some Hmong chose to leave as late as the 1980s. Others who did escape to refugee camps in Thailand shortly after the war hoped for the opportunity to return to Laos sometime in the future. Some families lived in refugee camps for more than 12 years hoping to be able to return home when it was safe. Still others stayed in Thai refugee camps hoping that the Thai government would eventually allow them to live permanently in Thailand so that they would not have to resettle in a third country (interview with D. Simon, diplomat with the American Embassy, Bangkok, Thailand, January 10, 1996).

According to Nancy Cummins, an administrator with the Joint Volunteer Agency (JVA) in charge of refugee resettlement in Thailand, the U.S. government felt a special responsibility to the Hmong people for their invaluable support and tremendous sacrifices during the Vietnam War and has continued to allow many Hmong people to resettle in the United States (interview, Bangkok, Thailand, January 10, 1996). However, opportunities for resettlement were coming to a close for the remaining Hmong in Thai refugee camps in the mid- to late-1990s. Both Edmonton (interview, Vientienne, Laos, January 19, 1996) and Simon (interview, Bangkok, Thailand, January 10, 1996) asserted that the remaining Hmong people in Thai refugee camps at that time were being pressured by the Thai government to make a decision to either resettle to a third country or repatriate to Laos.

Reflection Point 1.2

We have spent considerable time sharing Deng's cultural historical background. Why do you think it is important for teachers to understand the cultural historical backgrounds of the students in their classrooms? This question will be addressed throughout the book. (See Box 1.2 for a list of resources on language, culture, and teaching.)

Deng and his family, like many other Hmong from Laos, were caught up in a complex social, political, and economic web of circumstances that brought about their exodus from Laos to Thai refugee camps and eventually to the United States. Although Cindy asked Mrs. Moua about

---

Box 1.2
Resources on Learning About Language, Culture, and Teaching

Delpit, L. (1995). *Other people's children: Cultural conflict in the classroom*. New York: The New Press.

Florio-Ruane, S. (2001). *Teacher education and the cultural imagination*. Mahwah, NJ: Erlbaum.

Listen, D., & Zeichner, K. (1996). *Culture and teaching*. Mahwah, NJ: Erlbaum.

Minami, M., & Kennedy, B. (1991). *Language issues in literacy and bilingual/multicultural education*. Cambridge, MA: Harvard Educational Review.

Nieto, S. (2002). *Language, culture, and teaching: Critical perspectives for a new century*. Mahwah, NJ: Erlbaum.

Philips, S. (1983). *The invisible culture: Communication in classroom and community on the Warm Springs Indian Reservation*. Prospect Heights, IL: Waveland Press.

---

her family's decision to leave Laos for Thailand and the United States, she chose primarily to discuss details about the experience of leaving Laos and living in Thailand. She talked about a five-day journey on foot at night from the highlands of Laos to the Mekong River, where Deng and his family crossed from Laos to Thailand. In Thailand, Deng and his family lived in two different refugee camps for a period of about four years before the family moved to the midwestern United States.

Mrs. Moua stated that during the four years in refugee camps in Thailand, Deng attended school sporadically and part time and that instruction was in the Thai language. Phyllis Smith, with the United Nations High Commission on Refugees in Southeast Asia, and a former educational coordinator in one of the refugee camps in which Deng and his family lived, elaborated that students in the camps only attended school half-days and were instructed in three subjects: reading, Thai language, and math. Rote memorization of isolated skills was the focus of instruction (P. Smith, personal communication, January 19, 1996). Both Deng and Smith emphasized that teachers were very strict and that physical punishment was common when children misbehaved or did not have lessons memorized.

Although Deng's mother did not say explicitly why she and her four children settled in Michigan, we speculate that they chose it because some of Mrs. Moua's relatives lived there. Deng's family moved to a small, old apartment complex in downtown Lansing among other Hmong refugee families, and the children were bused to Oakland Elementary School. The apartment complex was in an area of town with a reputation for being somewhat dangerous and undesirable.

Organization of the Book

In this first chapter, we have provided valuable information about Deng's cultural historical background that you can draw upon as you read about his classroom literacy lessons. The remaining chapters in this book chronicle our learning as we listened carefully to Deng describe his understandings and interpretations of his experiences in literacy lessons in his classroom. We draw from this case of literacy learning, as well as pertinent scholarly literature and an exemplar ELL classroom, to explore the need for teachers to develop deeper understandings about (1) the role that cultural backgrounds and life experiences play in students' literacy learning, (2) the second-language acquisition process and its impact on students' literacy learning, (3) the learning and instruction required for children from diverse backgrounds, and (4) effective ways to structure classroom learning contexts and use literature and classroom materials.

Chapter 2 addresses the importance of developing and deepening teachers' knowledge base about language and culture. We further discuss what the education field stands to gain by listening to students. We draw from our work with Deng to contextualize these important conceptual ideas and provide concrete examples of ways that teachers can learn more about the cultural backgrounds of the students in their classrooms. Chapter 2 provides a backdrop for chapters 3 and 4 in which we look closely at Deng's literacy learning in his fifth-grade classroom.

Throughout the remaining chapters, we draw from Langer's (1984) notion of stances that readers assume as they navigate text. Langer suggests that as readers read texts, they *step into, move through, step back from,* and then *step out of* text worlds. In a sense, we take you through this same process with respect to Deng's story. In chapters 3 and 4, we step into and move through a close-up story of Deng's literacy learning during one period of lessons from his fifth-grade year in school. While working with Deng to study his learning in the context of one literacy unit, we noticed that different classroom participation structures influenced his literacy learning opportunities in different ways. Thus, chapter 3 explores Deng's literacy learning in whole-group settings, and chapter 4 focuses on his learning in small-group settings.

In chapter 5 we step back from the specific contexts we described in chapters 3 and 4 and look across those contexts to explore how the lessons we learned from them can inform our thinking about literacy instruction for ELLs like Deng. In chapter 6, we step out from Deng's story and look inside the classroom of a teacher who teaches many ELLs in an inner-city Chicago classroom. We provide concrete examples of how this teacher, Ms. Trost, enacts literacy instruction with her ELLs to meet their learning needs. Thus, in chapter 6, we draw from Deng's story, as well as related literature and experiences, to expose and interrogate our assumptions about learners, learning, and instruction for children from diverse backgrounds and explore concrete ways to enact meaningful instruction for ELLs in mainstream classrooms. Finally, we end chapter 6 by returning to Deng's story and discussing how all of us (Deng, Cindy, and Taffy) were transformed in the process of exploring Deng's literacy learning with him.

Chapter 2

Developing a Knowledge Base About Language and Culture

One evening, Deng, Vue, and Cindy are at Deng's apartment watching a videotape of Deng participating in a literacy lesson in his fifth-grade classroom. On the video, Deng and his 22 classmates are sitting on chairs in a semicircle in the front of the classroom around the teacher, Mrs. Weber, alternately reading and discussing the book Maniac Magee *(Spinelli, 1990). Sally has just taken a turn reading the following excerpt of text about the notorious Finsterwald—the mean old man in the story whom all of the children feared: "This, of course, was the infamous address of Finsterwald. Kids stayed away from Finsterwald the way old people stayed away from Saturday afternoon matinees at a $2.00 movie" (Spinelli, 1990, p. 16).*

Mrs. Weber:	*Why do adults avoid $2.00 matinees?*
Sally:	*'Cause kids are there!*
Mrs. Weber:	*How do kids typically act at afternoon matinees?*
Unison response:	*Loud and obnoxious!*

[As Deng, Vue, and Cindy watch the videotape of this lesson, Deng stops the tape to ask a question.]

Deng:	*Why adults stay away from $2.00 movie?*
Cindy:	*Why do you think that adults might not want to go to a $2.00 matinee movie?*
Deng:	*The movie not good?*

When Cindy asks Deng what a matinee movie is, he does not know. Together, Vue and Cindy explain that a matinee movie is an

15

inexpensive afternoon movie that mostly children would attend. Vue explains some ideas in Hmong that Deng appears not to understand in English, for example, that adults might not want to attend such a movie because children—undoubtedly attending the movie without many adults present—would probably be loud and unruly. Vue and Cindy ask Deng about his experience watching movies, and Deng says that he saw some movies in Thailand and that his family rents movies at home on a regular basis. Cindy does not think to ask Deng to describe the context of his cultural experiences with movies in Thailand—background information she could draw from to explain movie culture in the United States. During their conversation, Vue and Cindy discover that Deng has never been to a U.S. movie theater, and with the permission of Deng's mother, Vue and Cindy take Deng to a matinee movie several weekends later so he can experience a matinee movie.

On sharing this vignette (and other experiences with ELLs) with colleagues, we have heard a wide variety of interactions and interpretations, some of which we characterize as composite responses for which we offer commentaries. We use this vignette and our discussion of it as a springboard to discuss broader issues pertaining to language and culture that are relevant for teachers working with ELLs.

Reflection Point 2.1

1. In your journal, note your response to the vignette. Have you experienced a similar situation?

2. Read the respondent's reactions in Table 1 and note your response. Which reaction do you identify with more? Explain.

In our experience, most educators choose their profession because they are hard-working, dedicated, and caring people. However, even

Table 1
Different Responses to the Event With Deng

Respondent A	Respondent B
Well, you know, I often experience similar situations with other English-language learners. Unfortunately, they don't have many experiences or much background knowledge. You can see that Deng's teacher and some of his classmates did explain why adults wouldn't want to go to a matinee movie. Deng still didn't get it. I can't help but wonder if he really listened. I hate to say this, but, you know, as much as I want to, it is really hard to know how to help these kids.	Hmm...I have had many English-language learners, like Deng, in my classroom. When I have listened to my students tell, and write about, their life stories, I have discovered that they have unbelievable lived experiences. For example, many years ago, I had a student from Vietnam who described her family's escape from Vietnam after the Communist takeover. It was the stuff movies are made of! One of my struggles as a teacher is finding materials and developing lessons that all of my students can relate to. When I use stories like the Spinelli book [*Maniac Magee*] with my English-language learners, my challenge is to set up an instructional context where I provide enough scaffolding for my students to understand the story.

well-meaning people can have attitudes, dispositions, and knowledge that are not conducive to fostering student learning (Gay, 2000; Valenzuela, 1999). We become very concerned when we hear comments such as those made by Respondent A in Table 1. We ask ourselves, What does Respondent B know that Respondent A does not know about working with ELLs? That question is addressed in this chapter. First, we talk specifically about the event with Deng in light of the two respondents' comments. Then, we step back and discuss, more generally, how knowledge about language and culture can influence teachers' interpretations of instructional encounters with ELLs and shape the ways they make instructional decisions when working with them.

Interpreting Deng's and His Classmates' Reading of *Maniac Magee*

Sally and the other students who responded aloud to Mrs. Weber demonstrated that they knew most adults would not enjoy watching an afternoon movie with a theater full of unruly children. By understanding this information about movie viewing in U.S. culture and by knowing how to read analogies, Sally and some of her peers could infer from Spinelli's analogy that venturing into Finsterwald's backyard definitely was not something that children would want to do. Sally and her peers understood aspects of U.S. culture necessary to help them interpret the text in *Maniac Magee*. It is expected that members steeped in a language and culture would be able to draw from their tacit linguistic and cultural knowledge to interpret texts that reflect their cultural practices.

Deng, on the other hand, did not understand why adults would not want to attend a matinee, even after the teacher and some classmates explained the reason. Was this because Deng did not listen, as Respondent A suggested? We think that potential answers to this question are much more complicated. We do not think that knowledge exists within individuals' minds such that they either "have it" or "do not have it." For example, teachers and children should realize that attending movies is a cultural practice that may differ across countries and cultures. It would be problematic, in fact, to suggest that Deng has little or no experience with movies because Deng stated that he had seen movies in Thailand, and his family regularly watched videos of movies on their VCR at home. Also, if Cindy had asked about Deng's cultural experiences with movies in Thailand, she may have been able to draw from this background information to explain movie culture in the United States. What is at issue here is not Deng's understanding of the generic and decontextualized notion of *movie* but his experiences with the social practices (Garrison, 1995) associated with viewing matinees in the United States. Drawing from Gill (1993), we suggest that knowledge is "relational and participatory" (p. 3). Thus, in the specific example, individuals—such as Deng and his classmates—had different situated experiences with movie attendance from which to draw to interpret Spinelli's analogy.

In contrast, Respondent B understood that just because Deng did not have experience with U.S. cultural practices, such as matinees, it did not mean that he was deficient or had a deficit with respect to his knowledge of movies; rather, his cultural practices with movies were different from those of his U.S. peers. Respondent B understood that Deng and other ELLs like him bring rich and powerful cultural and linguistic resources that they draw on during their schooling. For example, English is Deng's fourth language, after Hmong, Thai, and Lao. Respondent B saw it as a responsibility to tap into and build on the rich cultural and linguistic resources of ELL students to help them achieve success in their U.S. classrooms. The ability to do this requires knowledge about language and culture as well as a disposition of openness as a learner.

The Complex Process of Acquiring an Additional Language

Anyone who has ever tried to acquire a new language undoubtedly has important insights into the difficulties involved in the second-language acquisition process. Scholars (e.g., Thomas & Collier, 2001; Wong Fillmore & Snow, 2002) suggest that it can take a minimum of five to seven years, or longer, to acquire proficiency in a new language. Many different factors influence the long, arduous, and complex process of acquiring a new language (see, e.g., Thomas & Collier, 2001). Teachers can control some of these factors, but not all of them. We share some of these factors and highlight areas where educators can make a difference in the unfolding of this process for ELLs.

Reflection Point 2.2_____

Take a few minutes to reflect on your own experiences trying to acquire a second language. If you have never been in that situation, please find someone who has and talk with that person about her or his experiences before addressing the following questions in your journal.

1. Have you ever tried to acquire a new language? If so, describe the context, including where you were and what you were doing. How were you treated? What did you find helpful, and what hindered your language learning?

2. Have you ever tried to use or been immersed in a new language? What were the consequences if you did not learn the language?

3. Compare your experiences to Katherine Paterson's in the excerpt below. Which parts of her story do you identify with?

The following excerpt from _Gates of Excellence: On Reading and Writing Books for Children_ (1981), by celebrated children's book author Katherine Paterson, begins our discussion of the complexities of acquiring a second language.

> If sometimes today, I feel myself drowning in verbiage, I can remember clearly how it feels not to have any words. In those months after I went to Japan in 1957, I would often find myself being taken somewhere by Japanese friends, not knowing where I was going or whom I was going to see. When I got to wherever I had been taken, I would find myself surrounded by people who were talking and laughing away, but because I did not know their words, I was totally shut out. As I began to learn a few words, people would try with infinite, exaggerated patience to talk with me. And because my speech was so halting and miserable, they would try to help me, try to put words into my mouth, try to guess what on earth it was I was trying to convey. When I was finally able to get out a sentence near enough to Japanese so that my listeners could grasp what I was driving at, they felt sure I'd appreciate knowing how I _should_ have expressed that particular thought, and they would gently, firmly, and ever so politely, take my pitiful little sentence apart and correct it for me.
>
> I'm sorry to report that I was not grateful. I wanted to yell, cry, throw a tantrum. _I am not a fool!_ I wanted to scream. If only you could know me in _English_, you would see at once what a clever, delightful person I am. But, of course, I didn't say it. I couldn't say it. I didn't have the minimum daily requirement in either vocabulary or syntax. The first time I saw the play _The Miracle Worker_, I knew what had been happening to me in those days. It was the rage of those starving for words.

By 1961, after four years in Japan, I boarded a jet in Tokyo and land-
ed about twenty hours later in Baltimore. I was met by my parents and
one of my sisters and taken home to Virginia. Every night for many
weeks I would get out of the soft bed, which was killing my back, and
lie sleepless on the floor. I was utterly miserable. "These people," I would
say to myself, meaning my own family, "these people don't even know
me." The reason I thought my family didn't know me was that they did-
n't know me in Japanese.

You see, in those four years I had become a different person. I had
not only learned new ways to express myself, I had new thoughts to express. I had come by painful experience to a conclusion that linguists
now advance: language is not simply the instrument by which we communicate thought. The language we speak will shape the thoughts and
feelings themselves. (pp. 7–8, emphasis in original)

As Paterson's poignant words illustrate, acquiring a new language is
much more than an academic exercise; it is personal. The experience
can be alienating, uncertain, confusing, and humiliating. Language is
much more than merely a depersonalized tool we use to navigate our
surroundings. Our language is intimately intertwined with who we are—
with our identity (Rodriguez, 1989). An understanding of the personal
trauma that can pervade the second-language acquisition experience
can give greater empathy for the students in our classrooms as they
learn English.

Now, armed with background knowledge about the emotional di-
mensions of learning a second language, we turn to Deng's language
acquisition story. When Deng arrived in the United States, he enrolled
in the last three months of third grade and spent all of fourth grade in a
mainstream classroom. When we met Deng, he had just begun fifth
grade and had been in the United States for about a year and a half.
Given that it takes five to seven years to become proficient in a new
language (Thomas & Collier, 2001; Wong Fillmore & Snow, 2002), Deng
was in the beginning phases of the language acquisition process when
we met him. By the end of fifth grade, when he read *Maniac Magee*, he
had only been learning English for two years. What factors influence
the second-language acquisition process for Deng and other ELLs? We
discuss answers to this question next.

Students' first-language literacy affects their second-language literacy
(Cummins, 2001; Krashen, 2003). For example, if students can read and

write in their first language, those literacy skills transfer to the new language. If, however, students cannot read and write in their first language, they must learn to read and write (and learn other content area subjects as well) while they are learning their new language. Under these circumstances, the task is daunting, and, as previously stated, it takes five to seven years to acquire academic proficiency in a new language. In Deng's case, he had limited schooling in Thai before coming to the United States. While in the Thai refugee camps for four years, Deng attended school sporadically and only during a portion of the day (rather than the whole day as in U.S. schools). In addition, schooling practices were didactic and punitive and involved rote memorization, with little or no emphasis on critical thinking. The only subjects addressed were reading, writing, and math in the Thai language.

Schooling conditions during the second-language acquisition process are also important. Optimal conditions for learning a second language include high-quality, dual-language programs whereby students acquire language and academic content in both their native language and their new language (Thomas & Collier, 2001). Paterson's vignette helps to illustrate why high-quality, dual-language programs are so helpful for ELLs. In the initial stages of learning a new language, the language learner does not know the new language well enough to communicate effectively or understand complex concepts or ideas in the new language. Because it takes five to seven years to acquire proficiency in the new language, second-language learners fall way behind their peers who continue to study and learn academic content while ELLs strive to master the language of instruction as well as academic content. Unfortunately, dual-language programs are not available in many U.S. schools and districts. In fact, recently, states such as California, Massachusetts, and Arizona have passed laws that limit bilingual education programs (Cummins, 2001). A discussion of the political backlash against bilingual education is beyond the purview of our work in this book. For more information on bilingual and ESL programs, see Box 2.1.

Before discussing the language support that was available to Deng, we want to make an important distinction in the second-language acquisition process that is useful background knowledge for teachers. While students are in the process of acquiring a new language, they

---

Box 2.1
Resources on Bilingual and ESL Programs
and the Second-Language Acquisition Process

Faltis, C., & Hudelson, S. (1998). *Bilingual education in elementary and secondary school communities: Toward understanding and caring*. Boston: Allyn & Bacon.

Harklau, L. (2000). From the "good kids" to the "worst": Representations of English language learners across educational settings. *TESOL Quarterly, 34*, 35–39.

Krashen, S.D. (1982). *Principles and practices in second language acquisition*. Oxford: Pergamon Press.

McKay, S.L., & Wong, S.L. (1996). Multiple discourses, multiple identities: Investment and agency in second-language learning among Chinese adolescent immigrant students. *Harvard Educational Review, 66*, 577–608.

Peirce, B.N. (1995). Social identity, investment, and language learning. *TESOL Quarterly, 29*, 9–31.

Simons, J., & Connelly, M. (2000). *Quality ESL programs: An administrator's guide*. Lanham, MD: Scarecrow Press.

---

first develop communicative competence in the language. Cummins (2001) refers to this as basic interpersonal communication skills (BICS). Basic communicative competence refers to the ability to engage in informal conversation. Typically, most students develop BICS in the first year or two of acquiring the new language. Cummins refers to the ability to engage in more complex academic tasks in the new language as cognitive academic language proficiency (CALP). It takes many years to develop the ability to understand and express complex academic ideas in a new language. This, of course, is one of the reasons that quality dual-language bilingual education programs are so beneficial to ELLs. In such programs, while students are learning their new language, they are not falling behind in the same academic content that their peers are learning. The BICS/CALP distinction is essential for educators to understand because educators who are not familiar with the complexities of the second-language acquisition process might assume that a child who has basic interpersonal communication skills in the new language can also understand complex academic content in the new language. Operating from this erroneous assumption, teachers may not provide ELLs with the scaffolding they need to understand academic content during lessons.

What language support was available to Deng in his school? Unfortunately, there were no Hmong–English bilingual programs available in Deng's school district. However, ESL support was available. Typically, ESL teachers work with individual students or small groups, pulling the ELLs out of the regular education classroom to provide instruction in basic English skills (Thomas & Collier, 2001). Deng received ESL support the last three months of third grade and all of fourth grade. However, Deng's mother decided that he would not receive ESL support in fifth grade. Thus, in fifth grade, he spent the entire school day in his mainstream English-speaking classroom with no language support of any kind. Where did that leave him? It left him where many ELLs are in U.S. classrooms—working with mainstream classroom teachers who may or may not have background and expertise to work with students who are learning a new language. Given the long, complex, and arduous second-language acquisition process, Deng had a long way to go. This was not because he did not work hard and put forth tremendous effort in school; on the contrary, his teacher, Mrs. Weber, said that Deng was one of the hardest working students in her classroom. Clearly, he was motivated to learn English and succeed in school. In order to be successful in school, however, he needed a great deal of help and support from caring and knowledgeable teachers.

We have just shared some important background information about second-language acquisition as well as Deng's location in the second-language acquisition process. However, as we alluded to earlier (e.g., with Deng's interpretation of the Finsterwald incident) and as Katherine Paterson suggested in the excerpt from her book that we included in this chapter, success in school requires much more than just knowledge of language on the part of the ELL. It also requires the support of caring and knowledgeable teachers. Teachers of ELLs must be open to explore the backgrounds, needs, and cultures of the ELLs in their classrooms. We now shift our discussion from Deng to ourselves as educators of ELLs. We begin the next section with a story to help us sort out how we, as educators, might think about framing our work with ELLs like Deng. This final section helps to set a context for how we approached our analysis of Deng's experiences in his fifth-grade classroom, which we discuss in chapters 3 and 4.

Being Open to Developing New Cultural Understandings

Suppose you've been having trouble with your eyes and you decide to go to an optometrist for help. After briefly listening to your complaint, he takes off his glasses and hands them to you.

"Put these on," he says. "I've worn this pair of glasses for ten years now and they've really helped me. I have an extra pair at home; you can wear these."

So you put them on, but it only makes the problem worse.

"This is terrible!" you exclaim. "I can't see a thing!"

"Well, what's wrong?" he asks. "They work great for me. Try harder."

"I am trying," you insist. "Everything is a blur."

"Well, what's the matter with you? Think positively."

"Okay. I positively can't see a thing."

"Boy, are you ungrateful!" he chides. "And after all I've done to help you!"

What are the chances you'd go back to that optometrist the next time you needed help? Not very good, I would imagine. (Covey, 1989, p. 236)

This story reminded us of a conversation that Cindy had with her sister—a high school health teacher in a small community in Oregon, where the student demographics have shifted significantly over the past 20 to 30 years. All the teachers in the high school were European American. Most of them were veteran teachers who had been teaching in the district for more than 20 years. When these teachers started their teaching careers, virtually all the students in the school were monolingual European Americans from lower middle to middle class backgrounds. Over the next two to three decades, many Latino families moved into the community, and the high school served large and growing numbers of Native American children from a nearby reservation. Many of the teachers in the high school lamented the fact that teaching just was not the same anymore. Many students in the school were not successful in their classes, and the dropout rate had increased. Teachers were frustrated. Students and their families were frustrated. Unfortunately, the school district did not recognize the need to make broad and sweeping changes in the ways in which it went about the business of educating the changing student population in its schools. Just as the optometrist in the excerpt tried to use the same pair of glasses for different people with different needs, the school district tried to use the same old educational practices and procedures for a student population that had changed dramatically.

The changing demographics in urban and rural school districts alike in U.S. public schools make it imperative for us as educators and administrators to recognize the need to adopt new lenses for engaging in our work as an educational community. What does it take to adopt these new lenses? First and foremost, it requires that we recognize a need to change. We need to realize that a pair of lenses for seeing and living in the world in one context or classroom with some students may or may not work in other contexts and classrooms with other students. In short, our ability to adjust our conceptual lenses in our work requires an understanding of the importance of attending carefully to our own dispositions and beliefs, as well as our own knowledge base (Major & Brock, 2003). It also requires that we listen to, and learn from, the students in our care. (See Box 2.2 for a list of resources for working effectively with ELLs.)

The following excerpt, taken from *Last Light Breaking: Living Among Alaska's Inupiat Eskimos* (Jans, 1993), helps illustrate important ideas to consider as teachers strive to listen to and learn from students. The excerpt is a conversational exchange between two people—a shopkeeper

---

Box 2.2
Resources for Teachers of ELLs

Books

Cary, S. (2000). *Working with second language learners: Answers to teachers' top ten questions.* Portsmouth, NH: Heinemann.

Diaz-Rico, L., & Weed, K. (2002). *The crosscultural, language, and academic development handbook: A complete K–12 reference guide.* Boston: Allyn & Bacon.

Freeman, D.E., & Freeman, Y.S. (2001). *Between two worlds: Access to second language acquisition.* Portsmouth, NH: Heinemann.

Spangenberg-Urbschat, K., & Pritchard, R. (Eds.). (1994). *Kids come in all languages: Reading instruction for ESL students.* Newark, DE: International Reading Association.

Website

New Teacher Center at UC Santa Cruz

www.newteachercenter.org

named Nick Jans (a European American male in his early 20s who later became an elementary school teacher) and a 4-year-old Inupiat Eskimo girl. Nick had recently earned a bachelor's degree and decided to leave his home state of Maine to explore life in remote Alaska. Almost out of money from his travels across Alaska, Nick assumed a position as a shopkeeper in a tiny, remote Eskimo village. The young girl was his very first customer. As you read, notice what Nick learned from listening to this child.

> A patter of footsteps announced my first customer—a skinny little girl, maybe four years old, with long black hair and a runny nose. She regarded the strange *naluaqmiu* before her with alarm. When I smiled, she steadied herself and solemnly laid a grubby handful of change on the counter, still eyeing me warily. In my best storekeeper's voice, I asked her what she needed today.
>
> Silence.
>
> "Candy?" I prompted.
>
> She didn't answer, but her eyes widened at the array behind the counter—cases of Milky Ways, Twizzlers, Drax Snax, LifeSavers, Garbage Can-dy—at least twenty varieties.
>
> "Which one?"
>
> More wide-eyed silence.
>
> "This one?"
>
> The child seemed to be on the verge of glaucoma.
>
> "What about this one?"
>
> Finally in exasperation I laid a Drax Snax and some Twizzlers on the counter and sorted out her change. With an expression of complete ecstasy the pretty little girl opened her mouth, exposing a row of blackened stumps. I'd just met my first candy junkie.
>
> It took me a couple of weeks to figure out that she'd been talking to me all along. The Inupiat are subtle, quiet people, and much of their communication hinges on nonverbal cues. Raising the eyebrows or widening the eyes means yes; a wrinkled nose is a negative. The poor girl had been shouting at me, "Yes! Yes! YES!" All these years later, I still recall that first simple failure to understand; it reminds me of all my failures since then and of the distance that remains.
>
> (Excerpted from *Last Light Breaking* by Nick Jans, © 1993, pp. 24–25, with permission of Alaska Northwest Books, an imprint of Graphic Arts Center Publishing.)

Last Light Breaking chronicles Nick's fascination with the Inupiat people—a people he grew to care deeply about as he lived and worked among them for many years. As previously mentioned, after his brief stint as a shopkeeper, Nick became an elementary school teacher. Prior to and during his work as a teacher of Inupiat children, Nick listened to—and learned from—them. In fact, many of Nick's most powerful learning experiences as a teacher came from the careful and thoughtful attention he paid to the students in his classroom.

Reflection Point 2.3

One reason that Nick was open to learning from and about the Inupiat was that he intentionally placed himself in a cultural and linguistic context vastly different from his prior experience. In a sense, he knew he had to alter his conceptual lenses, perspectives, or worldviews.

Have you ever been in a context (whether by choice or not) that caused you to "see" differently? If so, what precipitated your shift in perspective(s)? Remember you do not necessarily have to go to a different country or culture to be opened up to new and/or alternative insights or perspectives.

What lessons about literacy teaching and learning can we learn from Nick's story? Although there are many, we focus on the following two lessons: (1) the benefits of assuming the stance of an ethnographer in our own classrooms and (2) the importance of honing our communication skills as we engage in face-to-face interactions with others. Nick's encounter with the Inupiat child illustrates one of the central themes of this book. That is, there is much to be learned from really listening to students that can inform the ways that teachers design and implement literacy learning opportunities in their classrooms. Granted, Nick's learning experience occurred in a shop rather than a classroom, and he undoubtedly knew that he had much to learn about the Inupiat; however, teachers can have students from vastly different cultural and linguistic backgrounds in their classrooms, and, much like Nick, they need to see themselves as having much to learn from the children in their care.

In a sense, Nick assumed the stance of an ethnographer—one who seeks to understand the ways in which others experience the world (Geertz, 1973). This is a useful stance to assume in classrooms—especially when teachers work with students whose cultural and linguistic backgrounds differ from their own. Thus, good ethnographers have much in common with good teachers. That is, both seek to understand the conceptual worlds of others because teachers and ethnographers know that in order to engage in deep, meaningful, and sustained interactions with others, they must understand them—their beliefs, values, and ways of communicating (Eisner, 1998; Geertz, 1973; Wolcott, 2001). Good teachers have always known that quality teaching rests on knowing "where the learner is" and building lessons to capitalize on this information. We suggest that knowing where the learner is should include knowing about the learner's language and culture as well as the learner's prior knowledge with respect to academic content.

How do ethnographers learn to enter into the conceptual worlds of others? One of the most important conceptual tools that ethnographers employ is suspension of judgment while sorting out the perspectives of others (Eisner, 1998; Frank, 1999; Spindler & Spindler, 2000). For example, in the exchange between Nick Jans and the Inupiat child, Nick could have said to himself, "This child doesn't understand English/cannot communicate/is not very bright," or any number of other interpretations. Recall, for example, the easy answer that Respondent A gave for why Deng did not understand the classroom exchange (see Table 1 on p. 17). She said that he "just didn't listen." In Nick's case, rather than immediately passing judgment and assuming that he already knew the most feasible interpretation for his encounter with the child, he suspended his judgment temporarily and learned that the child was, in fact, communicating, but in a way that was not familiar to him. In addition to suspending judgment, Nick employed an approach that Au (1993) suggests is important when working with ELLs. That is, he assumed competence on the part of his conversational partner rather than merely assuming that she could not communicate.

Temporarily suspending judgment might be somewhat easier in contexts that are foreign to us, where we expect that our interpretations will be called into question. However, in contexts that are familiar—such as our classrooms—it can be much more difficult to even see the need to suspend judgment and question our perspectives and interpretations (Spindler & Spindler, 2000). Carolyn Frank, a teacher and ethnographer, talks about the difficulty of learning to see her classroom and students from a different perspective:

> I had to be wrenched away from my mainstream way of looking and my "one-way-only" of understanding the world. It was difficult to see life from a different viewpoint. The world was always OK for me without having to know from a different perspective. What I did not see was that the world was not OK for some others. (Frank, 1999, p. 4)

In the final sentence, Frank points to one of the very reasons we need to be open to seeing other viewpoints and worldviews. In the United States the public school system is designed to address the cultural perspectives, linguistic backgrounds, and educational needs of European Americans (Gay, 2000). Many scholars (e.g., Berliner & Biddle, 1995) argue that U.S. schools are, for the most part, successful in meeting the educational needs of the students for whom they were designed. However, as Frank points out, school may not work as well for students who are not European American. This observation is evidenced by a longstanding history of lower test scores for nonmainstream students on standardized tests of reading and writing (National Center for Educational Statistics, 1990, as cited in Jacob & Jordan, 1993), higher school dropout rates for children from linguistically and culturally diverse backgrounds, and an overrepresentation of diverse students in remedial programs and lower academic tracks in school systems (Oaks, 1985; Rose, 1989).

Reflection Point 2.4

What attempts have you made, or could you make, to listen to and communicate with ELLs in your classroom? What did you, or could you, learn from those attempts?

The main point that we have been making thus far is that listening means not only attending to others' words and actions but also attending to the ways in which we interpret others' words and actions. Our second point is that listening can be facilitated by the ways in which we communicate in face-to-face encounters. Gay (2000) argues that "effective communication is simultaneously a goal, a method, and the essence of quality classroom instruction" (p. xv). Communication with others—especially others who do not share common cultural and linguistic backgrounds—can be enhanced when we "seek first to understand, then to be understood" (Covey, 1989, p. x). Seeking to understand others requires *empathic listening*—seeking to understand others first—which is much more than merely hearing words. It involves "listening with your eyes and heart. You listen for feeling, for meaning. You listen for behavior.... You sense, you intuit, you feel" (Covey, 1989, p. 241). Recall, for example, that in order for Nick to really understand the small Inupiat child, he needed to notice and interpret her behavior, such as her facial expressions, and he needed to *want* to communicate with her and understand her.

Empathic listening is, of course, much easier said than done. Communicating with students from ethnically and linguistically diverse backgrounds may be problematic for European American teachers because misconceptions and confusions unintentionally can color interactions with students. Because our students may have cultural, linguistic, and social backgrounds that are vastly different from ours, we must be acutely aware that our beliefs, values, and norms for engaging in interactions may be very different from theirs (Gee, 1996). Further, because these differences can affect significantly our ability to communicate with them, they can also impact our ability to teach them. Covey (1989) reminds us that empathic listening is difficult. As in the story about the optometrist and the glasses, it is much easier to use the lenses we know and with which we are comfortable in our interactions with others. Covey (1989) says it best: "It's so much easier in the short run to hand someone a pair of glasses that have fit you so well these many years" (p. 242). The challenge for us as teachers is to adjust continually our conceptual lenses by listening carefully to students so that we can better educate them. In our work with Deng, we strove to understand how he experienced the literacy lessons in his fifth-grade classroom during whole-group and small-group instruction. In the following two chapters, we share what we learned about Deng's learning experiences in his classroom, where English was the medium of instruction.

Chapter 3

Whole-Group Instruction: Unique Challenges for English-Language Learners

One evening, Deng, Vue, and Cindy are sitting in Deng's living room watching a videotape of Deng as he participated in a literacy lesson. At one point in the lesson, Deng's teacher, Mrs. Weber, is reading aloud to the class a particularly poignant excerpt from Maniac Magee *(Spinelli, 1990). In the story, Maniac Magee—a homeless European American boy—has been adopted unofficially by the Beales—an African American family that lives on the east end of a town called Two Mills, Pennsylvania. Maniac notices that the people in this part of town refer to themselves as "black." Mrs. Weber reads an excerpt about Maniac's perceptions of those around him:*

> Maniac loved the colors of the East End, the people colors. For the life of him, he couldn't figure why these East Enders called themselves black. He kept looking and looking, and the colors he found were gingersnap and light fudge and dark fudge and acorn and butter rum and cinnamon and burnt orange. But never licorice, which, to him, was real black. (Spinelli, 1990, p. 51)

Mrs. Weber pauses briefly to tell the students that this is a significant passage. She explains that Maniac does not see people in categories of "black" and "white." Rather, he literally sees all people as having various shades of skin colors, and, figuratively, he sees them as individuals. Maniac does not place people in categories and then assign stereotypical attributes to each category.

33

As the class discusses this notion of skin tones, Mrs. Weber asks the students to move from their chairs to the center of the semicircle and put out their hands. Because the students are from a variety of ethnic backgrounds, there is an astonishing array of different colored outstretched hands in the center of the circle. Mrs. Weber talks with the students about the different colors of their hands and ends the episode by saying, "I have the feeling that the author wants you to know that Maniac spends time looking at the person rather than at the skin tone" (Brock, 1997, p. 121).

[Deng stops the videotape of this lesson.]

Deng: What is she mean put your hand out?

Deng and Vue speak in Hmong several times, and then Vue speaks.

Vue: She, she mentioned something about like put your hand out and stuff like that, and he doesn't understand. He wants to know what it means.

Cindy: [Looking at Deng] What does it mean for, are you asking what does it mean to put your hand out, or why is she asking you to do it?

Deng: Why is she asking?

Cindy: Ohhh. Good question, why is she asking the kids to do it? Can I, could I let you watch it for the next couple of minutes and then you can tell me why, why, what you think about that and then we can talk about it a little bit?

Deng: Yeah.

After they watch the rest of the brief segment, Cindy asks Deng to explain why he thinks his teacher asked the students to hold out their hands.

Deng: Because the teacher want to know the black and the white people their hands, what color are their hands.

Cindy: Are there any other reasons?

Deng: Because the teacher want to know what color the kids in the classroom are?

Deng and Vue then begin speaking in Hmong, and a few minutes later Deng adds that the teacher wanted the black people and the white people to be friends and not fight. Cindy asks Deng if he thought of that *idea by himself or if Vue helped him think of it, and Vue responds, "Actually, I just gave him some ideas. He knows that too, but I just gave him some ideas" (Brock, 2001, p. 471).*

This vignette illustrates three key ideas we use to frame this chapter. First, this lesson segment took place during a whole-group activity, which is the focus of this chapter. Whole-group instruction, common in many elementary classrooms—especially upper elementary classrooms (Tompkins, 2001)—can pose unique conceptual challenges for ELLs struggling to learn the language of instruction as well as the norms for classroom interactions in U.S. classrooms (Brock, McVee, Shojgreen-Downer, & Flores-Dueñas, 1998). Although Deng's class also participated in small-group activities (see chapter 4), most of the literacy instruction pertaining to the *Maniac Magee* text occurred during 18 whole-group lessons, each lasting approximately 40 minutes. Second, this chapter and the vignette are structured similarly. We discuss an event from Deng's classroom and then talk about Deng's interpretation of the event. We also share our interpretation of what occurred during the whole-group lessons and then shift to Deng's interpretations of the lessons as he watched them on videotape. Third, across this chapter we ask how careful reflection, from our perspective as well as Deng's, on a whole-group lesson format can inform teachers' understanding about using this participation structure with ELLs. In particular, we ask how students' different linguistic and cultural backgrounds can influence the ways they experience whole-group lessons in English and what teachers might do to make whole-group lesson structures more educative for ELLs.

Reflection Point 3.1

The focus throughout this book is on the learner learning. As you may have noticed, Deng found the classroom event in which the teacher asked to see the students' hands confusing. As you continue to read this chapter, think about what his reasons may have been. Also, consider how a close analysis of Deng's learning in his classroom can inform your thinking about work with other ELLs in other mainstream classrooms.

What We Noticed About Whole-Group Lessons

We begin with a typical whole-group literacy lesson in Deng's classroom. This sample lesson description serves as a backdrop against which we explore the nature of whole-group literacy lessons by asking three questions: (1) Who spoke during the lessons? (2) What did conversants discuss? and (3) How did conversants engage in the conversations?

During every whole-group lesson while reading the *Maniac Magee* text, students in Mrs. Weber's class sat on chairs in a semicircle around her in the front of the room. May 22 was their fifth day reading the text together. This 40-minute lesson was typical of most whole-group lessons in the classroom. At the beginning of each lesson, Mrs. Weber either reminded the students about a key topic or issue they had discussed the previous day, or she prompted them to consider a theme-related issue (e.g., homelessness, loneliness, prejudice). Sometimes she identified curricular goals (e.g., comprehension strategies, literary elements) she planned to discuss that day. For this lesson she indicated three focuses: (1) contrasts and conflicts in the story, (2) figures of speech used by the author, and (3) tall tales. Mrs. Weber, or a student she selected, then read aloud as students followed along, turning their pages in unison.

Mrs. Weber read about Maniac diligently helping Mrs. Beale with household chores such as doing the dishes, mowing the lawn, walking the dog, cleaning his room, and so forth. After reading several paragraphs, Mrs. Weber stopped and asked, "Are those all things that kids have to do within a household?" Several students responded in unison, "Nooo," and the class began a five-minute discussion about doing chores at home. During this conversation, two students made comments about their chores, and Mrs. Weber asked each of them a short series of questions that extended and clarified their initial comments. Additionally, Mrs. Weber talked about the importance of students assuming responsibilities around their homes, telling a personal story about doing household chores as a child. This pattern of interaction continued throughout the lesson: Mrs. Weber or a student read an excerpt from the story while the remaining class participants followed along silently in their own texts; the class discussed the excerpt for several minutes; and Mrs. Weber suggested that they continue reading the story.

Who Spoke During the Lessons, and What Did They Discuss?

Mrs. Weber's whole-group literacy lessons involved a series of ongoing conversations about segments of text in the story; however, a close look at the nature of the talk during these lessons revealed that very few students actually spoke during whole-group discussions. Table 2 provides an overview of the 22 class participants, in three target whole-group lessons on May 10, May 22, and June 5, to show who spoke and the number of times they spoke during lessons.

Reflection Point 3.2_____

In Table 2, notice which people in class were doing most of the talking. What other things do you notice? Jot down your observations and compare them to ours below.

First, we observed that Mrs. Weber consistently took the most turns speaking—approximately half—during the whole-group lessons. Second, only a small number of students actually spoke during these lessons: one European American girl (Sally) and three European American boys (Dan, Bill, and Chris). In fact, those five people took over 75% of all the speaking turns. Of the remaining responses, 25% were primarily unison responses: Mrs. Weber posed a question, and the students replied in unison. Half the students in Mrs. Weber's classroom were European American, a third were African American, and one sixth were Latino or Asian American.

Table 2
Participants' Speaking Turns During Whole-Group Lessons

Category	Name	Number of Turns May 10	Number of Turns May 22	Number of Turns June 5	Total Number of Turns
Girls	1. Sally	**28**	**48**	27	103
	2. Lisa	11	0	5	16
	3. Rashiya	7	absent	absent	7
	4. Shondra	1	0	0	1
	5. Reshaun	1	2	3	6
	6. Yesenia	1	0	0	1
	7. Kelly	0	1	0	1
	8. LeShon	0	2	2	4
	9. Lakisha	0	0	4	4
	10. Maria	0	0	0	0
	11. Larissa	0	0	4	4
Boys	12. Dan	**45**	**22**	15	82
	13. Bill	**17**	**10**	**4**	31
	14. Chris	**7**	**18**	**16**	41
	15. Miguel	7	3	4	14
	16. Cam	5	0	15	20
	17. Tran	5	1	7	13
	18. Don	1	absent	absent	1
	19. Ron	1	5	1	7
	20. Dusty	0	1	1	2
	21. Timothy	1	0	5	6
	22. Deng	0	0	14	14
Teacher	23. Mrs. Weber	**149**	**127**	**158**	434
Group Responses	24. Multiple students	29	19	39	87

Note. The number of speaking turns was determined by looking at the transcripts of each lesson and counting the number of times each person made comments during the lesson. Data for the speakers with the most speaking turns appear in bold. Some turns were longer than others, which is not reflected in the chart. Some turns involved either the teacher or students reading the story, whereas other turns pertained to actual comments about the story.

Although Table 2 shows who spoke during whole-group lessons, many questions were left unanswered about these lessons. For example, is it important that the few people who spoke during literacy lessons were all European American? Under what conditions might it be important? Specifically, was it important for Deng? How could we know? We delve more deeply into the nature of the lessons to address these questions—especially as they pertain to Deng. Next, we take a closer look at what the teacher and students discussed during their lessons as well as how they engaged in that talk. We begin by examining Deng's actual speaking turns.

Look closely at Table 2; notice that on June 5 Deng had 14 speaking turns. On that day, Mrs. Weber explicitly asked Deng to read aloud from the text, which was difficult for him. In the story, Maniac accepted a dare from several kids, agreeing to stay for 10 minutes in the backyard of Mr. Finsterwald—the mean man who hated kids. All the neighborhood kids—except Maniac—were terrified of Mr. Finsterwald. Mrs. Weber read aloud that a child named Russell was going to time Maniac's stay in Finsterwald's backyard. Russell was Maniac's friend and, as such, was very nervous about Maniac attempting this dangerous feat. After reading several paragraphs from the text, Mrs. Weber asked Deng to read. She began by pronouncing the name *Russell*, and Deng started reading at that point.

Deng: *Russell his...*

Mrs. Weber: throat...

Deng: *throat too dry to speak rai...*

Mrs. Weber: Raised his hand...

Deng: *raised his hand for, from 10 minutes, 15 kid and...*

Mrs. Weber: possibly...

Deng: *possibly the universe...*

Mrs. Weber: held their breath...

Deng: *held their breath. The only sound made inside their...*

Mrs. Weber: heads...

Deng: *head...*

Mrs. Weber: heads...

Deng: *heads...*

Mrs. Weber: Um hum.

(See also Brock, Moore, & Parks, 2003, p. 25.)

As Deng continued reading, Mrs. Weber helped him with most of the words in the few sentences that he actually read. There was no discussion about the content of the text. Rather, Mrs. Weber helped Deng to pronounce the words in the text. She provided a great deal of assistance—even to the point of making sure that he pronounced the *s* on the word *heads*. This was the only time Deng ever spoke aloud during any of the 18 whole-group lessons in the unit. Deng never once spoke voluntarily in the whole group during the reading or discussion of *Maniac Magee*.

You may be saying to yourself, "Yes, but I would never *not* call on an ELL in my classroom during so many whole-group lessons, and if I did I would not focus only on his or her pronunciation of the text." Although most teachers have only the best intentions when working with the ELLs in our classrooms, we may engage inadvertently in behaviors that are not helpful for these students (Valenzuela, 1999). Gay (2000) asserts, for example, that the kind of "assistance" that Mrs. Weber provided to Deng is typical for teachers of ELLs; that is, much of the reading instruction for ELLs in mainstream English-speaking classrooms involves work with low-level skills such as pronunciation.

We wish to point out that lesson segments such as the one just described were actually quite rare during the lessons pertaining to *Maniac Magee*. For example, there was only one other time when Mrs. Weber helped a child who was having difficulty reading aloud pronounce the words in the text. Typically, the conceptual content of lessons was much richer than in the lesson segment with Deng.

Reflection Point 3.3

Notice that Mrs. Weber—not the students in the class—raised the questions and issues for discussion during the whole-group lesson segments we have presented. Think about what impact this may have had on Deng's learning as you continue to read.

How Did Mrs. Weber and the Students Engage in Discussions During the Lessons?

In this section, we present another lesson segment and elaborate further on how Mrs. Weber's class engaged in class discussions. The class was discussing how Maniac had run away from the home of his feuding aunt and uncle and was now homeless. Mrs. Weber and her students discussed options for where Maniac might have found food and shelter. They suggested that he might have slept on a park bench, in a tunnel, under a bridge, and so forth. Mrs. Weber made the comment that their responses revealed that they were not from the country, and then Sally suggested that perhaps Maniac could sleep in a barn.

Mrs. Weber:	Sure, in any of the outer buildings on a farm. I would usually go to a place where I might find farm animals. Why?
Miguel:	For food?
Mrs. Weber:	Well, maybe for food, but more than food.
Chris:	Um, but, I don't know what to call a horse's bedroom really. A trailer? A horse's trailer?
Mrs. Weber:	Maybe a horse trailer. OK, why else?

The conversation continued until Lisa suggested that someone might want to find a place next to an animal in order to stay warm from the animal's body heat, and Mrs. Weber responded, "That's right!"

Reflection Point 3.4

After reading this vignette carefully for a sense of how Mrs. Weber and her students engaged in talk, write down what you noticed to compare with what we noticed about interactions during these whole-group lessons.

Upon close examination of this segment, as well as the conversations across the 18 whole-group lessons, we noticed that many of the conversational turns involved the I-R-E sequence (Cazden, 1988). That is, Mrs. Weber *initiated* (I) a brief discussion, a student (or students) *responded* (R), and then Mrs. Weber *evaluated* (E) the student responses. We labeled Mrs. Weber's first comment as both an "evaluation" and an "initiation." She suggested that Sally's comment was on track (i.e., "Sure") and then elaborated on why her comment made sense. Then Mrs. Weber asked a question to initiate further comments and ideas from the students. Thus, there was both an evaluation and an initiation in Mrs. Weber's turn. Miguel and Chris both responded to Mrs. Weber's original initiation. Mrs. Weber evaluated each of their responses as viable, but, clearly, they were not the responses she was seeking. She continued to initiate additional comments until Lisa commented about an animal's body heat, and Mrs. Weber affirmed that this was the response she was seeking. The conversation then moved on to a different, but related, topic.

As the segment of conversation indicates, and as Cazden (1988) notes, the I-R-E pattern is not always rigidly in place for conversants. Yet, it is clear from the lesson segment, as well as the number of turns Mrs. Weber took as illustrated by Table 2, that she did most of the initiating and evaluating and the students did most of the responding during whole-group lessons. The issue of who initiates, responds to, and evaluates comments within conversations is important with respect to ELLs. The fact that the I-R-E pattern is in place means that the students primarily respond to the teacher's issues, concerns, and questions pertaining to the text rather than their own. This, of course, is not a problem if the teacher's and students' concerns and questions are similar. If the teacher and the students come from different cultural backgrounds, and if the students are in the process of learning the language of instruction, chances are good that they would have very different questions, concerns, and understandings of the text. Issues such as how conversations are structured and who is sanctioned to speak affect who has access to the conversation, what gets discussed, who influences the ongoing discussion, and, perhaps most important, what students have the opportunity to learn.

After studying the 18 whole-group videotaped lessons, watching carefully, and rewatching the three target whole-group lessons in Table 2, we offer a brief recap of what we noticed about how Mrs. Weber and her students interacted during the lessons. Mrs. Weber asked many questions that were almost always addressed to the student audience in general; rarely did she address a question directly to a specific child. Thus, it seemed like anyone could assume the conversational floor. In reality, however, Mrs. Weber and only a few students did almost all the talking. In fact, European American students—mostly boys—spoke most during whole-group lessons. When students did speak, they did not pose the questions; rather, their conversational turns involved displaying knowledge. Typically, they tried to answer the teacher's questions with the "correct" answers.

Reflection Point 3.5

Based on our discussion above and your own interpretation of the interactions in Mrs. Weber's classroom, what kinds of intellectual challenges do you think Deng faced? Please draw from your own experiences with ELLs to frame your response.

What Deng Said About Whole-Group Lessons

In order to explore Deng's interpretation of his experiences in whole-group lessons, we examine his comments about the three lessons listed in Table 2 that occurred at the beginning, middle, and end of the *Maniac Magee* unit. As Deng, Vue, and Cindy watched these lessons together, Cindy's only directions to Deng were to stop the videotapes at any place he wished to make comments and to speak in either Hmong or English—whichever language he felt most comfortable using. When Deng stopped the tapes to make comments or ask questions, Cindy asked probing questions to gain a sense of how he interpreted the lessons he watched. The vignette at the beginning of this chapter provides an example of the kinds of discussions the three (i.e., Deng, Vue, and Cindy) had during the lesson viewings.

What we learned about Deng's interpretation of the lessons shocked us. The first 40-minute lesson tape was stopped 28 times: 4 times by Vue, 1 time by Cindy, and 24 times by Deng. Five of the times the tape was stopped, they discussed procedural issues such as "How much longer is this lesson?" or, more commonly, Deng or Vue asked Deng's younger brother to stop talking while they watched the tape. During 4 times the tape was stopped, Deng expressed what he understood about the lesson, but 19 of the times the tape was stopped, Deng expressed confusion about something in the lesson. He wondered why the class was engaged in a particular activity (e.g., Deng had no idea why his teacher asked the class to show the colors of their hands in the introductory vignette), about a character or event in the story, about a discussion the class was having pertaining to the book, and about the meaning of a word from either the book or the class discussion about the book.

The following two whole-group lessons they watched together proceeded like the first one, with a similar pattern of times and reasons Deng stopped the videotape. For example, during the second whole-group lesson, he stopped the tape 8 times for procedural questions or concerns, 7 times for something he understood, and 16 times for something that was confusing. Thus, Deng was confused over 50% of the times he stopped the tape. Similarly, during the third lesson, Deng was confused about something in the lesson or the story approximately 80% of the times he stopped the tape.

Deng revealed that he was confused about much of what occurred during the lessons. In order to provide additional insights into the nature of Deng's confusions during the lessons, we share one example of a conversation between Deng, Vue, and Cindy at one point when Deng stopped the videotape. In *Maniac Magee*, Maniac was homeless because his parents had been killed and he ran away from the home of his feuding aunt and uncle. Over the course of the story, Maniac lived with many different people such as the Beale family and an old man named Grayson. At this point in the story, Maniac lived with the McNab family. The family's lifestyle and household were both deplorable. There were several unclean and undisciplined children of various ages with a drunken father and no mother. The house was always filthy and unsanitary. The two youngest McNab children were twins named Russell and Piper. Not surprisingly, Russell and Piper did not attend school regularly, and their father did little to encourage them to attend school. Maniac was a good influence on the boys and got them to attend school by bribing them. He primarily bribed them to go to school by getting them pizza on Fridays, but the boys were tiring of this particular bribe and decided to request something else. In the following segment, Mrs. Weber and students Chris and Bill discuss Mr. McNab, and then Mrs. Weber resumes reading.

Mrs. Weber: What was his [referring to Mr. McNab] big thing?

Chris: Drinking beer.

Bill: [overlapping speech] Drinking beer and going out.

Mrs. Weber: Drinking beer, and "do your homework." He never sat down and said, "What can I help you with?" [Mrs. Weber resumed reading from the text.] "And so when Maniac tried to cut the next pizza deal, Russell answered, 'No!' 'No?' echoed Maniac who had been afraid it would come to this. 'No,' said Russell. 'We want something else.' 'Oh?' said Maniac. 'What's that?' They told him, if he wanted another week's worth of school out of them, he'd have to enter Finsterwald's backyard and stay there for ten minutes. Piper shuttered at the very thought. When Maniac casually answered, 'Okay, it's a deal,' Piper ran shrieking from the house" (Spinelli, 1990, p. 25).

As Deng, Vue, and Cindy watched this part of the lesson, Deng stopped the tape when the teacher mentioned Finsterwald's name.

Deng: Who are Finster?

Cindy: I'm sorry? [Cindy wasn't sure what Deng was asking.]

Deng: Finster.

Cindy: Who is Finsterwald?

Deng: Yeah.

Cindy: Um, Finsterwald was um, he was that man that lived in the neighborhood, and he was very mean. Do, do you know what *mean* is?

Deng: Yeah.

Cindy: Can you tell, can you tell us?

Deng: Like bad people?

Cindy explained more about Finsterwald, how he was a scary man who was feared by all the children in the neighborhood. She then asked Deng why Maniac was going to go in Finsterwald's backyard. He responded, "To try what happen?" Cindy was intrigued by Deng's comments for several reasons. First, she expected that Deng already knew who Finsterwald was because Spinelli had included him in the story from the very beginning. Also, Deng, Vue, and Cindy had discussed Finsterwald during a previous viewing of a taped lesson. Thus, even though Finsterwald was not a new character in the story and he had been discussed before, Deng was still not sure who he was or how he fit into the story.

Second, because Deng chose to stop the lesson at a place other than where the teacher stopped the story to discuss it, this led us to wonder how many other questions or confusions Deng had about the story that might not have matched the times the teacher stopped reading the text to discuss the story.

Finally, Cindy suspected that Deng was not clear about why Maniac was going to spend 10 minutes in Finsterwald's backyard. As they continued watching the lesson, Deng stopped the tape to ask if Maniac was currently living with the McNabs. Cindy asked him to speculate as to whether or not he thought Maniac lived with the McNabs. He said that he suspected that Maniac did live with them because he remembered hearing the teacher read about Maniac, Russell, and Piper playing in the basement of the McNab's home. Cindy then asked Deng why he thought that Maniac went into Finsterwald's backyard.

Deng: To try to see what happen.

Cindy: To see what would happen?

Deng: Yeah.

Cindy: Did...Who wanted him to be there? Did he want to be there or did somebody else want him to be there?

Deng: Think somebody else.

Cindy: Do you...do you know who it was?

Deng: Russell.

Cindy: Russell and Piper?

Deng: Yeah.

Cindy: What, and why did they want him to go there?

Deng: To try...

Cindy: and see what would happen?

Deng: Yeah.

This discussion led us to believe that Deng understood some of the particulars about the event in the story in which Maniac spent 10 minutes in Finsterwald's backyard. Deng knew that Maniac lived with Russell and Piper (although his earlier question to Cindy indicated that he was not sure about this) and that they wanted him to enter Finsterwald's backyard. We suspect, however, that Deng did not understand the nuances of the event. We question whether Deng understood that Maniac spent 10 minutes in Finsterwald's backyard on a dare in order to bribe Russell and Piper to go to school. Also, we suspect that Deng did not understand why Russell and Piper might ask Maniac to engage in such a feat in the first place. The author alluded to the fact that Russell and Piper were elevated in the eyes of their friends (15 children from the neighborhood watched this daring feat) because they had the power to get Maniac to do what any other child in that context would consider unthinkable—actually enter and spend time in Finsterwald's backyard. These points help illustrate how understanding the nuances of a character's actions and the events in which they participate requires a great deal of knowledge about the culture in which the story is situated; that is, it is possible to take for granted the extensive cultural knowledge required to comprehend stories.

As another example of the crucial role that cultural background knowledge plays in interpreting texts, recall the poignant excerpt from *Maniac Magee* about various shades of black and Mrs. Weber's request for the students to compare the colors of their own hands. In further discussion of that vignette, we make several points about Deng's interpretation of the event and pose key issues that Deng's interpretation of this classroom event raises for us as educators.

Perhaps the first and most significant point to note is that Deng identified the activity as confusing. It was not clear to him why Mrs. Weber wanted the students to look at and discuss the different shades of their hands. Even after viewing the entire discussion segment, Deng believed that Mrs. Weber asked the students to engage in the activity only to look at the colors of their hands. He seemed to interpret her use of the word *see* literally. Although Deng interpreted this event literally, others (including the teacher, Vue, and Cindy) interpreted it figuratively; that is, those individuals privy to a particular way of schooling (i.e., the expectation that one thinks figuratively about texts) knew that the activity was not about the teacher looking at the colors of the students' hands.

A second key point is that the cultural cues students draw from to make sense of texts can vary significantly and shape the ways in which they read texts, including the actual books they read and the interactions in class about those books. For example, it may be that Deng did not understand the event because he did not understand the issue of racism in the United States, particularly the history of racism between blacks and whites. Many students in Mrs. Weber's classroom undoubtedly had learned about Martin Luther King Jr., Rosa Parks, and other important U.S. citizens who fought peacefully for the rights of African Americans. Deng's take on racism may have been different from U.S.-born students in Mrs. Weber's class who knew about racism in the United States. Whatever understandings brought to bear on Deng's interpretation of this lesson segment, however, this difference in "seeing" or interpreting school-related events could signal a crucial difference between ELLs such as Deng being "in" the system and knowing what's intended and participating on the margins (Brock, 1997). (See the resources in Box 3.1 for many ways to use multicultural literature in the classroom.)

Box 3.1
Multicultural Literature Resources for Educators

Ballentine, D., & Hill, L. (2000). Teaching beyond once upon a time. *Language Arts, 78,* 11–20.

Cai, M., & Sims Bishop, R. (1994). Multicultural literature for children: Towards a clarification of the concept. In A.H. Dyson & C. Genishi (Eds.), *The need for story: Cultural diversity in classroom and community*. Urbana, IL: National Council of Teachers of English.

Harris, V. (Ed.). (1997). *Using multiethnic literature in the K–8 classroom*. Norwood, MA: Christopher-Gordon.

Norton, D.E. (2001). *Multicultural children's literature: Through the eyes of many children*. New Jersey: Merrill Prentice Hall.

Rogers, T., Soter, A., & Sims Bishop, R. (Eds.). (1996). *Reading across cultures: Teaching literature in a diverse society*. New York: Teachers College Press.

Willis, A.I., & Johnson, J.L. (2000, September). "A horizon of possibilities": A critical framework for transforming multiethnic literature instruction. *Reading Online, 4*(3). Available: http://www.readingonline.org/articles/art_index.asp?HREF = /articles/willis/index.html

Wollman-Banilla, J.E. (1998). Outrageous viewpoints: Teachers' criteria for rejecting works of children's literature. *Language Arts, 75,* 287–295.

We believe that this lesson segment raises two important issues for teachers:

1. Potential cultural miscues are difficult for teachers who are members of the mainstream culture to tease out for ELLs in their classrooms. Cindy was actually in Deng's classroom as the lesson with the hands unfolded. Her initial response was that it was an impressive and powerful learning event for the students. Mrs. Weber had, in her opinion, masterfully related events in the story to students' personal lives. By having the students compare their own skin color, she drew them into Spinelli's discussion about different shades of skin color and the problems of attributing people's character to the color of their skin. Cindy also felt that Mrs. Weber had discussed important ethical and moral issues pertaining to racism and prejudice with the students. Finally, by the manner in which she helped the students interact with the story, she seemed to be striving to help them personally connect with the events and

people in the story. Only by listening to Deng did we understand that his experience was far different from what Cindy had described in her notes. Although all the wonderful things in her notes may have happened for some students, they did not happen for Deng.

2. This issue is closely related to the first one: Good teaching is not context free; it is culturally sensitive. That is, Cindy's initial interpretation of this event focused on the nature of the strategies and activities to determine good teaching. She fell into the seductive trap of assuming that good teaching is transcendent (Gay, 2000). Gay suggests the following:

> Many educators still believe that good teaching transcends place, people, time, and context. They contend it has nothing to do with the class, race, gender, ethnicity, or culture of students and teachers. This attitude is manifested in the expression "Good teachers anywhere are good teachers everywhere." Individuals who subscribe to this belief fail to realize that their standards of "goodness" in teaching and learning are culturally determined and are not the same for all ethnic groups. (p. 22)

One problem with that attitude is that it focuses on the process of teachers teaching rather than on learners learning (Lave, 1996). That is, while the activity with the hands in Mrs. Weber's classroom may have worked conceptually for some students in the class, it did not work for Deng. He had no idea what he was supposed to learn from the activity. Thus, as Gay (2000) warns, it is problematic to judge the merits of the activity absent a discussion of what specific students learned or did not learn from it. As humans, we are steeped in our own cultural ways of seeing. When teachers' cultural ways of seeing are different from those of their students, they must exercise diligence about striving to see through the eyes of the ELLs in their classrooms. If teachers are to really meet the learning needs of ELLs, they must "learn to see what we have learned not to notice" (Eisner, 1998, p. 77).

What does all of this have to do with Deng? Because so few different students actually spoke during whole-group lessons, it is clear that silence during whole-group lessons was considered an acceptable way to participate. Deng's silence during all 18 whole-group lessons, except when the teacher called on him directly, could be considered successful engagement in the conversation if physical behavior during lessons met the criteria for successful engagement. Why? Because Deng looked like he was engaged and understanding during whole-group lessons. That is, he attended to the person speaking, and he appeared to follow along in his text when students or the teacher read. However, because Deng only chose silence as a way to participate, it was not possible to know by merely watching whether he and other silent students were actually learning during ongoing whole-group conversations. However, viewing Deng's silence in the context of his reported confusion about whole-group lessons during viewing sessions, it is reasonable to assume that he was mostly confused during whole-group lessons. This may have been true for other students as well. A central way for teachers to assess the learning and understanding of their ELLs is to give them myriad opportunities to write and talk during lessons. When ELLs are silent during extended periods of lesson times, it is not possible to know if or how much they are learning from lessons. In the next chapter, we explore Deng's literacy learning opportunities in a different participation structure: small groups.

Chapter 4

Small-Group Instruction: Applications to Deng's Learning

It is the last day of fifth grade for Deng and his classmates and the last day for discussing Maniac Magee *(Spinelli, 1990). Today, Mrs. Weber had asked the children to get into their small groups to discuss the following topics about the book: homelessness, racism, loneliness, tall tales, realistic fiction, contrasts, favorites, and how the story changed them. Deng is in the same small group he has worked with on five other occasions to write or talk about* Maniac Magee. *The other members of the group are Tran, a Korean American boy, and Chris, a European American boy. The boys have been discussing homelessness, which Tran feels they have covered well enough. Tran wants to move to racism, the next topic on the chalkboard.*

Tran:	*See, OK, homelessness, OK, that part solves it. OK, racism. I mean, why don't they just get together instead of making stuff up about each other? I mean, racism is bad.*
Chris:	*Yeah, Fishbelly's bad.*
Tran:	*I know. Because people, they don't know about each other so just, they just make stuff up about each other. I mean, what do you think about racism, Deng?*
Deng:	*Wh...what is that mean?*
Tran:	*What?*
Deng:	*What is that mean? What is racism?*

Tran's first comment above ended the discussion of the previous topic (homelessness), introduced the next topic (racism), asked a question about racism in the text, and made a statement about racism. Chris's response about "Fishbelly" refers to the derogatory name that Mars Bar (an African American character in the story) often called Maniac (a European American character) before he and Maniac became friends. In his next comment, Tran explicitly invited Deng into the conversation. At that point, Deng indicated that he did not understand the term *racism*.

This dialogue illustrates one of the significantly different ways in which Deng experienced small-group conversations as compared to whole-group lessons. During whole-group lessons, Deng never voluntarily spoke, and during viewing sessions of the lessons, Deng indicated that he had been confused most of the time. However, as the vignette illustrates, Deng did speak up during small-group activities. Throughout this chapter, we elaborate on this and other ways in which Deng and his classmates participated in small-group discussions as well as the impact that these kinds of interactions had on Deng's learning.

First, we discuss Deng's interpretations of the taped small-group activities. Second, we share our interpretation of what occurred during focus small-group activities. Third, across the chapter we explore how careful reflection, from our perspective as well as Deng's, can inform understanding about ELLs' experiences in small groups. In particular, we ask how the nature of interactions within small groups can support, or not support, children's learning. Finally, we ask how a close analysis of Deng's learning in this particular classroom context can inform teachers' thinking about work with ELLs in their own classrooms.

Reflection Point 4.1

After reading about Deng's participation in whole-group literacy lessons (see chapter 3), make a prediction about Deng's participation and learning in small-group work. What do you anticipate Deng's learning and experiences will be in small-group interactions? Why?

Overview of Small-Group Activities

Mrs. Weber's students engaged in small-group activities six times during their reading of *Maniac Magee*. Four of the activities involved students writing in their journals and two activities involved discussions (see Table 3). As the students engaged in these activities, Mrs. Weber encouraged them to think of one another as potential resources or sources of information; for example, while students wrote, she encouraged them to engage in relevant talk about what they were writing. (See Box 4.1 for resources on small-group instruction.)

Table 3 provides a brief overview of the six small-group activities. The first three columns indicate the number, name, and length of each activity. The final column provides a brief description of each activity. The fourth and sixth activities were the longest and most academically rigorous activities, so Cindy took videotapes of Deng participating in those activities to his house for him to watch and comment on. During his viewing of the Character Map Activity, in particular, Deng had at lot to say about the role his peers played in helping him understand *Maniac Magee*. Thus, we use that discussion as a backdrop to discuss Deng's interpretation of small-group activities. We look across both focus activities—but primarily focus on the Discussion Activity—to render our interpretations of what occurred for Deng in small-group activities.

Box 4.1
Managing Small Groups and Resources for Small-Group Instruction

Cohen, E. (1994). *Designing group work: Strategies for the heterogeneous classroom*. New York: Teachers College Press.

Ford, M.P., & Opitz, M. (2002). Using centers to engage children during guided reading time: Intensifying learning experiences away from the teacher. *The Reading Teacher, 55*, 710–717.

Gambrell, L., & Almasi, J. (Eds.). (1996). *Lively discussions! Fostering engaged reading*. Newark, DE: International Reading Association.

Gambrell, L., Morrow, L.M., Neuman, S., & Pressley, M. (1999). *Best practices in literacy instruction*. New York: Guilford Press.

Roser, N., & Martinez, M. (1995). *Book talk and beyond: Children and teachers respond to literature*. Newark, DE: International Reading Association.

Table 3
Overview of Small-Group Activities

Activity Number	Name of Activity	Length of Activity	Description of Activity
1	Journal Writing	10–12 minutes	Prediction about what might happen next in the story
2	Journal Writing	10–12 minutes	Prediction about what might happen next in the story
3	Journal Writing	10–12 minutes	Prediction about what might happen next in the story
4	Character Map	25 minutes	Character map about Grayson, an important character in the story
5	Oral Summary	10 minutes	Discussion of the main events from the day's reading
6	Discussion	34 minutes	Summary discussion of major story themes

What Deng Said About Small-Group Activities

During the first two to three minutes of the Character Map Activity, Mrs. Weber asked the children to make a character map of Grayson, a character recently introduced in the story. Maniac had just left the Beale family, whose home was vandalized because they allowed a white boy to live with them in their black neighborhood. Because Maniac loved the Beales too much to see anything bad happen to them, he ran away. After living alone at the zoo for a while, Maniac was adopted by Grayson, an old man who worked at a local baseball park.

Mrs. Weber modeled the activity by drawing a character map on the chalkboard. She asked the students to include five words on their character maps to describe Grayson's personality. The children were instructed to find at least two pieces of evidence from the story to support their choice of adjectives. Deng worked with Tran and Chris on this activity. Figure 2 illustrates the final product the children created.

Later as Deng, Vue, and Cindy watched the videotape of the activity, Deng stopped the 25-minute Character Map Activity tape only once, to comment on his appearance on tape; he said that he looked tired that day. Because Cindy had encouraged Deng to make comments and ask questions, she was perplexed that Deng had stopped this videotape only once—he had stopped the videotape of the whole-group lesson the previous week 24 times. As soon as the tape was over Cindy asked Deng about this issue.

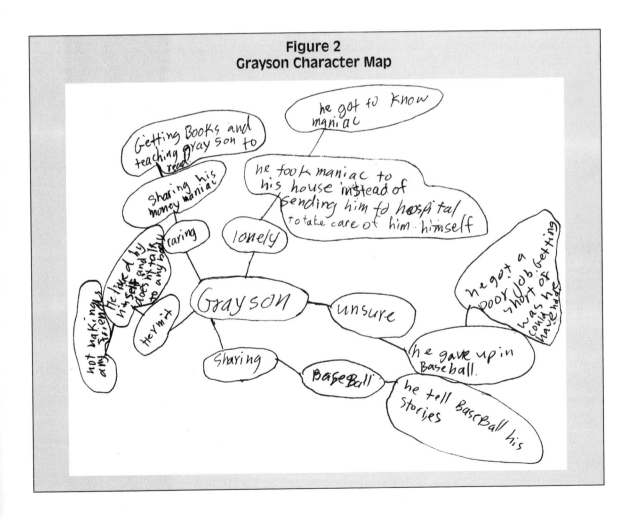

Figure 2
Grayson Character Map

Cindy: [To Deng] Could I ask you some questions?

Deng: Yeah.

Cindy: Now, I noticed that, um, remember last time you watched a video, the one with the hands in it? Do you remember that?

Deng: Yeah.

Cindy: Um, it seems like you were asking...to stop the video a lot, but this time you didn't. Can, can you tell me why you didn't? Why did you want to stop a lot the other time but not this time?

Deng: Because the other time, I don't understand.

Cindy: The other time you didn't understand?

Deng: Yeah.

Cindy: Oh, you were asking us to stop because you didn't understand?

Deng: Yeah.

Cindy: But what happened this time?

Deng: I understand.

As Deng's comments illustrate, his interpretations of the small-group and whole-group activities were quite different. During the viewing of the small-group activity, he felt that he had understood the text he was reading; that is, he both said and demonstrated by the manner in which he chose to control the viewing session that he understood what was happening in the small-group activity, whereas, in the whole-group lesson the week before, he had been confused most of the time. Cindy was curious as to why he felt that he understood the small-group activity so much better than the whole-group lesson.

Cindy: So this time you understood? Can you tell me why you understood this time and not last time?

Deng: Because me and Chris and Tran talking.

Cindy continued to ask Deng about his different perceptions of the whole-group lesson and the small-group activity. Most of Deng's comments related to what he found helpful about the small group. For example, Cindy asked Deng what the teacher wanted the boys to do in the small-group Character Map Activity, and he said that she wanted them to learn about Maniac and Grayson.

Cindy: So, what she wanted you to do was to learn about Maniac and Grayson and talk about them? Why did she have you do it in groups, I wonder.

Deng: Um, because maybe if you don't know, one of the group know.

Cindy: Ohh, so maybe somebody in the group doesn't know and then people in the group can help each other?

Clearly, Deng felt that talking with his peers in small groups was useful, emphasizing that students could help one another if something was not understood. Deng added that the boys told him what was happening in the story, and they further explained the assignment to him as they worked on it. However, in whole groups his experience was primarily listening.

Cindy wondered about the reasons for Deng's different interactions in the small group as compared to the large group. She made the following observation:

Cindy: Actually, I noticed something interesting. I noticed that in the big group you didn't raise your hand to ask questions, but in that little group you did ask questions.

Deng: Yeah.

Cindy: You did? What kinds of questions did you ask them?

Deng: About what they doing.

Cindy: About what they were doing?

Deng: Yeah.

Cindy: Did you ask any other kinds of questions?

Deng: Yes, but I forgot.

Cindy: But you forgot? OK. How come you asked questions in that little group but not in the big group?

[Deng did not respond right away, and Vue spoke briefly in Hmong.]

Deng: Because we are friends.

Cindy: Oh, you're friends with the two boys?

[Deng and Vue spoke briefly in Hmong, and Cindy asked Vue what he had said to Deng.]

Vue: I was asking him, like, it seemed like, he still shy to work in groups, but he said, no, that he participate more cuz they kind of like friendly with him and stuff like that, you know.

Deng emphasized the helpful manner in which he and his peers interacted. He felt comfortable interacting with Chris and Tran because they were his friends and because they did not "talk too fast" or use "hard" words. In contrast, Deng said that in the whole group the teacher often talked too fast and used words he did not understand. Further, he felt uncomfortable making comments in the large group because he felt that he did not know English very well, and he described himself as shy with others.

We found Deng's discussion of the differences between whole- and small-group participation fascinating. Because we know from the literature that small groups are not always effective learning contexts for children (e.g., Paratore & McCormick, 1997), we really wanted to try to find out why this particular small group worked for Deng.

What We Noticed About Small-Group Activities

We noticed obvious differences in who spoke and how much they spoke during small-group activities and during whole-group lessons. During the Character Map and Discussion activities, Deng actually spoke (see Table 4), which stood in stark contrast to his participation in the 18 forty-minute whole-group lessons in which he never spoke a word voluntarily. Although Table 4 provides a sense of the number of turns that Deng, his classmates, Mrs. Weber, and Cindy took during Deng's small-group activities, it does not reveal the nature or complexity of the conversations. We discuss some of our observations here and more in the following section.

First, although Mrs. Weber also contributed on both days, and Cindy made a few comments during the second activity, the students—Deng, Tran, and Chris—took the responsibility for developing and discussing their ideas within their group. Second, Tran spoke almost half the time, Chris spoke just over a third of the time, and Deng spoke just under a

Table 4
Number of Speaking Turns Taken in Small-Group Activities

Category	Name	Number of Turns: Character Map Activity	Number of Turns: Discussion Activity	Total
Boys	1. Tran	76	149	225
	2. Chris	52	103	155
	3. Deng	23	67	90
Adults	4. Mrs. Weber	8	2	10
	5. Cindy	0	3	3

fifth of the time. Thus, in terms of conversational turns, Tran appeared to be the leader in the group. Third, the boys' contributions to the conversation in the small group were almost the opposite of their contributions to the whole-group lessons. For example, Tran rarely, if ever, spoke during whole-group lessons but contributed most during small-group activities. Chris, one of the four children in the large group who consistently contributed the most during whole-group lessons, contributed considerably less than Tran during small-group activities. Deng, who rarely spoke—and never voluntarily—during whole-group lessons, took almost a fifth of the speaking turns during small-group activities. In the following, we focus on *what* was discussed during each small-group activity and *how* participants interacted.

How Deng, Tran, and Chris Engaged in Small-Group Discussions

We briefly introduced the Discussion Activity at the beginning of this chapter; however, before we discuss at length our interpretation of the boys' interactions during the activity, we want to elaborate on the atmosphere of Mrs. Weber's classroom at the time. The activity occurred on the last day of the school year, but in spite of that, students were excited about reading *Maniac Magee* and readily turned to the final activity of the unit. Having completed the book the previous day, students were eager for the chance to discuss it with one another. Although Mrs. Weber knew the students were anxious to talk about the book, she also knew it was her last opportunity to provide guidance in helping them explore the thematic and substantive issues in the book. She directed the students to consider the following areas in their discussions: homelessness, racism, loneliness, tall tales, realistic fiction, contrasts, favorites, and how the story changed them. She told them that while she wanted each of them to address these general areas, they could decide how to structure their conversations.

When we left Deng and his two peers in the vignette at the beginning of the chapter, Deng had just asked what was meant by the term *racism*. Prior to Deng's question below, Tran had asked Deng directly what he thought about racism in the story *Maniac Magee*.

Deng: What is that mean? What is racism?

Tran: It means when people don't like another person.

Chris: It's like when a person—

Tran: [overlapping Chris's comment] Like, let's, OK—

Chris: [overlapping Tran's comment] when a white person and a black person don't get along.

Tran: Or another culture.

Chris: Yeah, yeah, or another culture. But it's mainly white and black. And a white person doesn't like a black person because that person's black.

Tran and Chris had suggested that *racism* meant that people from different cultures did not like each other. Chris asserted that it usually occurred between blacks and whites. After defining racism for Deng, Tran sought Deng's input about what they had just said. Chris, however, was not finished talking about racism as primarily a conflict between blacks and whites.

Tran: Yeah, what do you think about that Deng?

Chris: A white person thinks, you know, a black person is not as good as them.

Tran: Yeah, what do you think Deng?

Deng: I think Amanda don't like—

Tran: I mean, do you think it's good, bad?

Deng: No, is ba, bad.

Tran: Yeah, it's bad, right Deng? It's…OK, racism is bad. And Maniac, and Maniac, Maniac had to go through lots of racism through his, where he was.

When Tran asked Deng's opinion about racism, Deng started to draw a character (Amanda Beale) from the text into his explanation. Tran clarified that he just wanted to know, in general, whether Deng thought racism was good or bad. When Deng answered (appropriately, from Tran's perspective), Tran began to tie the issue of racism back to the text—he suggested that Maniac had to deal with lots of racism. In the following conversation, Chris mentions some of the racist characters with whom Maniac interacted such as Mars Bar (a teenage African American male), John McNab (a teenage Caucasian male), and Grayson (an elderly Caucasian male).

Chris: With Mars Bar and John McNab.

Tran: And everybody else, but—

Chris: [overlapping speech] I don't know about Grayson, though, was he—

Tran: [overlapping speech] But I think after Maniac visited both sides, I think they did fine on racism. He can bring 'em together. OK, loneliness.

Tran ended by suggesting that Maniac interacted with racist and nonracist people from the East End of town (i.e., the black side) and the West End of town (i.e., the white side), and Maniac was able to bring the two sides together.

Reflection Point 4.2

Consider the several small-group dialogues and what they reveal about how the boys interacted. What did you notice about the specific ways that Tran, in particular, used various different conversational moves to help Deng understand the definition of racism?

First and foremost, Tran and Chris took Deng's confusion about racism seriously. They defined racism, scaffolded Deng's understanding of racism by drawing him into the conversation and making it clear that racism is a bad thing, and related racism back to the characters in the story. In addition, Deng seemed comfortable asking the boys about things that were confusing to him. Tran, in particular, seemed interested in scaffolding and checking for Deng's understanding. For example, the boys provided examples of racism, and then Tran asked Deng what he thought about what they were saying. We do wish that Tran had encouraged Deng to further expand on his ideas when he mentioned Amanda Beale; instead, Tran directed Deng back to whether racism was good or bad. In general, however, we were impressed with the ways in which Tran, in particular, seemed to act as Deng's teacher and advocate during small-group conversations.

Often, the ideas that Deng shared or the suggestions that he made during small-group interactions were in direct response to Tran's questions. Tran played an important role in inviting Deng into the conversation, and he often made it clear that he valued Deng's ideas, opinions, and thoughts. The following excerpt illustrates how Tran expertly brought Deng into the conversation, elicited his opinions and ideas, and gently nudged and guided his thinking:

Tran: Anything else why you liked the book? Or homelessness or whatever? [Looking directly at Deng] What do you think about Maniac?

Deng: I think, I think Maniac want to be like the best family.

Tran: He wants the best family?

Deng: Yeah.

Tran: Oh, that's good.

Deng: And he want to have mother and dad and sister and brother.

Through his questions, Tran got Deng to express his understanding of Maniac's loneliness: Maniac desperately wanted to be a part of a loving and caring family. Not only did Tran elicit Deng's understanding of that, he also pushed Deng to think about what happened at the end of the story.

Tran: Do you think he got the best family?

Deng: No.

Tran: The Beales?

Deng: Yeah, yeah. [Deng's voice tone seemed to indicate that he was acquiescing to Tran's ideas.]

Tran's last question above could be interpreted to mean that he was puzzled by Deng's response that Maniac did not get the best family. At the end of the story the previous day, Amanda Beale and Mars Bar found Maniac at the zoo where he had been living, and Amanda insisted that Maniac come back to live with the Beale family. Maniac agreed. Maniac loved the Beale family, and they loved him. Further, Maniac would have parents and siblings. Undoubtedly, Tran was confused by Deng's negative comment given that the class had just learned the day before that Maniac would have a family again. Tran's question may have prompted Deng to change his response to "Yeah, yeah." In other words, because of Tran's question Deng may have realized that Maniac would indeed live with a good family. Tran continued to question Deng:

Tran: Oh, OK. Do you think they're the best family for Maniac?

Chris: Nobody's the best family.

Deng: Maniac...no, maybe Grayson.

Tran: Yeah, Grayson. Maybe if Grayson, maybe had kids, that'd be another song.

Deng: Yeah.

Deng's suggestion that Grayson would be a good family for Maniac was a clever and sophisticated response to Tran's probing question, given the context of the story. Earlier in the story, Maniac was unofficially adopted by Grayson, an elderly gentleman, and lived with him until Grayson died.

Deng's comment showed that he understood that Maniac and Grayson were like family and loved each other. (Recall that Tran, Chris, and Deng had made a character map of Grayson several weeks earlier.) Deng agreed with Tran's suggestion that Grayson would be an even better family for Maniac if he had children, presumably so Maniac would have siblings.

As we looked closely at Deng's participation in the small-group discussions, we noticed that almost half of his contributions involved making suggestions and sharing ideas. He also agreed with the ideas of others, sought help and clarification when he was confused, and clarified points that had already been mentioned. It was both interesting and important for us to note that small-group conversations were not only about Deng needing help or clarification; he also made important contributions to the boys' ongoing conversations, such as "I think, I think Maniac want to be like the best family." Thus, Deng's role during the conversations was multifaceted and complex. Other patterns emerged when we looked closely at the boys' conversations: Tran often controlled access to the conversational floor and the flow of the conversation, and he often acted as Deng's advocate during the conversations.

A striking similarity across both small-group viewing sessions was that, unlike in the whole-group viewing sessions, Deng rarely suggested that he was confused. The numbers of times Deng indicated confusion during each different type of participation structure differed markedly: once during the 25-minute Character Map Activity and three times during the Discussion Activity, as compared to dozens of times during whole-group lessons.

Deng also participated actively by speaking and writing during small-group activities, whereas, he listened passively during large-group lessons. Deng explained that he chose to interact more in small groups because he was more comfortable in that setting. That is, he felt that because he was friends with Tran and Chris, they would help when he did not understand something, they would use words that he could understand, and so forth. In contrast, in the large group, he was often unfamiliar with the words Mrs. Weber used, uncomfortable with his level of English proficiency, and too shy to speak in front of so many people.

Deng's small-group activities varied significantly from whole-class lessons. In whole-group lessons, all students needed knowledge of the

Maniac Magee text, knowledge of U.S. culture, and knowledge about whole-group interactional norms in order to participate successfully. In Deng's small group, however, knowledge of the text and U.S. culture were not prerequisites to successful interactions within the group. In fact, in the small group it was acceptable to reveal confusions about the story and U.S. culture. Further, the nature of the interpersonal interactions amongst the boys influenced the understandings constructed as they worked through assigned tasks.

We wish to point out, however, that not all small-group contexts for ELLs are equal—nor are small-group contexts necessarily always, or usually, useful to promote the learning of ELLs. Rather, the nature of the interactions within an instructional setting is key to the quality of student learning that happens there (Gutiérrez, 1992, 1994). The small-group context worked for Deng for the following reasons:

- Mrs. Weber spent considerable time teaching her students to interact effectively with peers in small groups. For example, the students had recently worked together in small groups for several weeks to create a project. An important component of the project was daily self- and group evaluation of their participation in small groups.

- Mrs. Weber did not assign formal roles to the students for their small-group work; rather, she wanted her students to engage in meaningful and authentic dialogue during their small-group work. Earlier in the year as students were learning to work in small groups, they discussed regularly how to work effectively with peers, including such important topics as settling disputes and questioning others to engage them in the discussion.

- Mrs. Weber selected the students who would work together in a group. Undoubtedly, she knew that Tran would be an advocate for Deng and work effectively with him.

In this chapter we discussed in depth Deng's participation in two small-group activities. In the next chapter, we draw on Deng's experiences and ask how a close look at Deng's literacy learning opportunities can inform our thinking about the broader context of working with ELLs in mainstream classrooms.

Chapter 5

Evaluating and Reflecting on Deng's Learning

*I*n chapters 3 and 4, we stepped into and began moving through an in-depth description of Deng's literacy learning experiences in whole-group lessons and small-group activities during the reading lessons for *Maniac Magee* (Spinelli, 1990). While some of the activities and experiences Deng had in his classroom promoted his learning, others were far less effective. In this chapter, we look more closely at Deng's experiences in whole-group lessons and small-group activities, exploring the following questions: What worked and why? and its corollary, What did not seem to work and why not? In doing so, we continue moving through Deng's overall literacy learning experiences reflecting on relationships between Mrs. Weber's instructional decisions and Deng's learning experiences—thinking in terms of both decisions that promoted his learning and ones that contributed to his confusion during literacy lessons.

Moving Through: Instructional Analysis Using Three Principles

Deng's words and actions illustrate how much he valued the small-group interactions around the text *Maniac Magee*, specifically because he believed they were helpful in promoting his learning. Deng articulated three reasons the small-group settings were valuable: (1) He felt more comfortable talking in a small group because Tran and Chris were his friends; (2) he felt comfortable sharing his confusions within the small group; and (3) Tran and Chris responded to his expressions of confusion with information that helped him to make sense of the concepts. As we noted in chapter 4, it was no accident that Deng's small group functioned successfully for him. Mrs. Weber spent considerable time that year teaching Deng and his classmates how to interact effectively in small groups to support one another's learning. Further, she drew on her knowledge of her students' abilities and personalities, as well as their friendship circles, in creating their small working groups.

In contrast, as illustrated in chapter 3, Deng's words and actions demonstrated the confusion he often experienced in whole-group lessons. Recall that during whole-group lessons Mrs. Weber led the class lessons using a common participation structure in U.S. education, referred to as an Initiate-Respond-Evaluate (I-R-E) discussion pattern (Cazden, 1988). The teacher initiates an interaction, a student (or students) responds, and the teacher evaluates the response. Mrs. Weber *initiated* questions. A student (or students) *responded*. Overwhelmingly, only a few students responded to Mrs. Weber's questions. Then Mrs. Weber *evaluated* the students' responses. The I-R-E pattern is not inherently a problem (see, e.g., Wells, 1999), but it does have limitations. As we see in this setting, it can (a) lead to the teacher doing most of the talking, with only a few students participating; (b) limit the depth of responses that any contributor makes; and (c) limit the degree of information the teacher has for assessing the understanding of students, such as Deng, who are silent. Table 5 provides an overview of some of Mrs. Weber's instructional practices that proved to be problematic for Deng and also suggestions for what she might have done to shape the classroom interactions to better meet Deng's needs as a learner. For example, it may have seemed like anyone could assume the "conversational floor" to answer Mrs. Weber's questions, but in reality Mrs. Weber and a few of her European American students did almost all of the talking—Deng had been socialized in Asian schools not to assume the conversational floor unless called upon by the teacher.

Turning to the research literature, we can begin to unpack why Deng found the small group to be more supportive of his learning. Scholars (e.g., Gee, 2003; George, Raphael, & Florio-Ruane, 2003; Hudelson, Poynor, & Wolfe, 2003; Tharp, 1997) emphasize the following three gen-

Table 5
Analysis of Whole-Group Instruction

What Mrs. Weber Did	What Mrs. Weber Might Have Done Differently
• Asked most of the questions during whole-group lessons. • Usually addressed questions to the student audience in general; rarely addressed a question directly to a specific student. • Did most of the talking, along with a few European American students. • Encouraged the "correct" answers to questions. When students did speak, their conversational turns involved displaying knowledge. Typically, they tried to answer the teacher's questions with the "correct" answers.	• Encouraged the students to pose their own questions to the group. • Called on specific students so that lots of students were invited to talk during whole-group lessons. • Employed an informal system (such as giving each student a turn-taking artifact) to monitor students' contributions to the conversation. With turn-taking artifacts, once each student has taken a turn, she or he must wait until others have had their turn to talk before contributing to the conversation again. • Set up a system to encourage students to pose their own questions and confusions about the story. Encourage think–pair–share minidiscussions during whole-group lessons whereby students could express to a partner what they thought about a particular issue and/or what they wondered about. Explicitly ask students to raise their questions and confusions with the larger group. • Assessed prior knowledge regarding the key topics she was addressing in class. This would have given her a sense of what Deng and his classmates knew and needed to learn relative to the topics she covered in class.

eral principles of instruction that teachers must consider in order to foster the learning of ELLs:

- Types of activities and the settings in which the activities occur
- Nature of interactions afforded within the settings
- Opportunities to assess students' understandings

In Tables 6–8, we address these three principles as they relate to Deng's experiences in small-group activities and whole-group lessons.

First Principle: Structuring Classroom Activities

Teachers working with ELLs in their classrooms should structure classroom activities that are intellectually challenging, reflect high expectations for student literacy learning, and encourage students' ownership of literacy.

Reflection Point 5.1

As you read Table 6, look at similarities and differences between small-group activities and whole-group lessons. Once you have identified similarities and differences, what do you consider to be most significant about them?

Table 6
Structuring Classroom Activities: Examples From Deng's Small Group and the Whole Class

Participation Structure	Key Events	Mrs. Weber's Actions	Beliefs Reflected in Mrs. Weber's Actions
Small-Group Activities	• Deng, Tran, and Chris talked and wrote about story elements such as character, plot, and setting. • All three boys offered their interpretations of the story and made connections between the story and their own lives.	• Provided time, space, and structure in her classroom schedule for some small-group work. • Structured activities (e.g., the Character Map and Discussion activities) that were focused, interesting, and intellectually challenging.	• Students need to understand elements of literature (e.g., character development, plot, setting). • Students need to connect personally to the stories they read. • The teacher must provide explicit, and meaningful, instruction pertaining to literacy skills and strategies and the social practices associated with reading and writing.
Whole-Group Lessons	• Mrs. Weber and several students (e.g., Sally, Dan, and Chris) talked and wrote about story elements such as character, plot, and setting. • Mrs. Weber and several students (e.g., Sally, Dan, and Chris) offered interpretations of the story and made connections between the story and their own lives.	• Most of the time devoted to reading lessons in Mrs. Weber's classroom involved whole-group discussions of *Maniac Magee*. • These discussions centered on important story elements as well as connections that Mrs. Weber and some students were making to the text.	• Students need to understand elements of literature (e.g., character development, plot, setting), and they can do this by listening to others talk about these topics. • Students need to connect personally to the stories they read, and they can do this by listening to others talk about personal connections to the text.

In contrasting the small- and whole-group contexts, we noticed first, in both contexts, Mrs. Weber made it a point to address aspects of story elements and story structure. Additionally, she strove to have her students engage personally with the text *Maniac Magee*. Clearly, as an overarching goal, Mrs. Weber was interested in helping Deng and his classmates develop high levels of literacy. Also, as an ELL in Mrs. Weber's classroom, Deng engaged in classroom activities *with* his classmates and was not pulled aside to engage in low-level skill-and-drill instruction until he became proficient in English, a practice all too common in U.S. classrooms (Hudelson, Poynor, & Wolfe, 2003).

Second Principle: Structuring Students' Interactions

Teachers should promote ELLs' literacy learning by structuring effective dialogic interactions in a variety of contexts between novices and experts in a community of learners.

Reflection Point 5.2

Table 7 focuses on the nature of interactions in Deng's small-group and whole-group literacy lessons. What do you notice about the differences for Deng in the nature of interactions between the small-group activities and the whole-group lessons?

The most striking difference to us between the small-group activities and whole-group lessons is the level of activity of the students in each setting. In the small-group context, we saw highly active learners—a stark contrast to their more passive performance during whole-group lessons (Gee, 2003). Instruction (and subsequently Deng's learning opportunities) seemed to break down in the whole-group context. Here, Mrs. Weber appeared to operate on the assumption that the explicit instruction (in the form of explanations and questions) and the responses offered by a somewhat limited number of students would be sufficient to support the learning of all of the students in the group. When Deng's

Table 7
Structuring Students' Interactions: Examples From Deng's Small Group and the Whole Class

Participation Structure	Key Events	Mrs. Weber's Actions	Beliefs Reflected in Mrs. Weber's Actions
Small-Group Activities	• Deng had the opportunity to experiment with his developing understanding of English in a meaningful context with the assistance of his more knowledgeable English-speaking peers. • Deng had the opportunity to sort through confusions pertaining to *Maniac Magee* with his peers who were genuinely interested in fostering his understanding of the story.	• Spent considerable time across the year teaching her children to interact effectively together without the teacher always present. • Earlier in the year, developed self-evaluation protocols for her children to use to assess their small-group behavior and that of their peers. • Across the year, provided instruction so that the students knew what to do in their small-group interactions pertaining to *Maniac Magee*.	• Students need the opportunity to talk and write together to sort out their understandings of the story and story meanings. • The teacher must provide explicit instruction in how to interact effectively in small groups. • Literacy is much more than a set of discrete skills pertaining to reading and writing. Through reading, writing, and talking, children can learn to construct and justify rich and varied interpretations of texts.
Whole-Group Lessons	• Deng listened as Mrs. Weber and a few of his peers discussed the text *Maniac Magee*. • Discussions involved a limited number of students answering Mrs. Weber's questions about the text. Their answers were displays of knowledge about the story and/or their connections to the story. There were no opportunities for Deng, or his classmates, to make public their confusions about the text.	• Used the I-R-E pattern to engage a limited number of students in a discussion of the text. • Did not require the students to raise their hands to respond to her questions; rather, when she posed a question, a student (typically Sally, Dan, or Chris) just assumed the conversational floor and began to answer her question.	• Extensive use of whole-group instruction is an effective way to teach literacy in an upper elementary classroom. • The teacher must provide explicit instruction by lecturing about aspects of the story, and asking students questions about the story. • Students who don't participate orally in the whole group can understand the focus of the lesson by listening.

interactions shifted from active, personal involvement in the small groups to listening in the whole group, his learning opportunities waned. Deng's whole-group context did not promote the kinds of deep engagement with literary texts that teachers want for their students. (See Box 5.1 for innovative resources on engaging ELLs.)

Surface-level engagement with texts can involve—among other things—passive listening with no mechanisms to check for developing understandings or confusions. This is what happened to Deng during whole-group lessons. Because Deng only listened during whole-group lessons—and there were no mechanisms to check for Deng's understanding—Mrs. Weber had no way to know if what Deng heard during whole-group lessons made any sense to him. Another example of surface-level engagement with texts involves manipulating words or syntax to produce answers to literal questions, for example, as in assignments that require students to provide literal answers to questions in social studies or science texts. Students may be asked to write out an answer to a question such as "What is photosynthesis?" Merely by finding the definition either in the glossary or in the body of the science text, they can write out the definition without demonstrating a meaningful conceptual understanding of photosynthesis.

According to Gee (2003), if we want to change the nature of classroom talk and subsequent understandings, we have to change the kinds of activity settings for students' learning. Activity settings that demand more active learning can militate against shallow understandings of

---

Box 5.1
Innovative Approaches to Teaching ELLs

Ada, A.F. (2003). *A magical encounter: Latino children's literature in the classroom*. Boston: Allyn & Bacon.

Boyd, F., & Brock, C.H. (with Rozendal, M.). (2004). *Multicultural and multilingual literacy and language: Contexts and practices*. New York: Guilford.

García, G. (2003). *English learners: Reaching the highest level of English literacy*. Newark, DE: International Reading Association.

Peregoy, S.F., & Boyle, O.F. (2004). *Reading, writing and learning in ESL: A resource book for K–12 teachers* (4th ed.). Boston: Allyn & Bacon.

academic content. Gee (2003) suggests that active learning involves the following three things: "forming new *affiliations*, *experiencing* the world in new ways, and *preparation* for future learning" (p. 32). "Forming new affiliations" refers to understanding an academic domain in ways that insiders understand the domain. For example, Chris and Tran understood U.S. culture as well as reading and discussing stories from an insider's perspective. By sorting out—and sorting through—confusions, questions, and textual connections pertaining to *Maniac Magee* with Tran and Chris, Deng, too, could begin to understand the text as an insider. To begin to develop insider ways of making sense of text, however, Deng needed to experience (i.e., operate in and on the world) in meaningful ways—through talk, reading, and writing with the assistance of others when confusions (such as the definition of racism) arose. Experiencing was much more than passive listening for Deng in the small group. He actively constructed writing and talk that was made public for his peers to respond to during small-group interactions. By actively writing and talking about the story with his peers in his small group, and then receiving input from them about his talk and writing, Deng was also preparing for meaningful future engagement with stories. That is, what Deng learned about story structure, story elements, U.S. culture, and so forth, could be applied to other readings of other texts.

Active engagement opportunities for assessment were missing in whole-group lessons for Deng and worked against his learning. (See Box 5.2 for a list of practical resources for instruction in mainstream classrooms.) First, Mrs. Weber needed to restructure the ways in which she asked Deng and his classmates to engage with the text, *Maniac Magee*, during whole-group lessons so that they were actively engaged with making sense of the text (see the examples provided in Table 5 on p. 69). Second, as a passive listener, Deng was unable to provide Mrs. Weber with anything on which to evaluate his understanding. Thus, she could not—and did not—assess his learning during the 18 whole-group lessons. She had no idea what sense he was making of the whole-group lessons. Mrs. Weber might have addressed these two concerns by encouraging the students—at reasonable intervals during the whole-group lesson—to turn to a peer and share what they are thinking about the lesson. After giving the students a few minutes, at most, to do this, she could then ask for vol-

---

Box 5.2
Practical Resources for Instruction in Mainstream Classrooms

Au, K.H., Carroll, J., & Scheu, J.A. (1997). *Balanced literacy instruction: A teacher's resource book.* Norwood, MA: Christopher-Gordon.

Harvey, S., & Goudvis, A. (2000). *Strategies that work: Teaching comprehension to enhance understanding.* York, ME: Stenhouse.

McLaughlin, M. (2003). *Guided comprehension in the primary grades.* Newark, DE: International Reading Association.

Rasinski, T.V. (2003). *The fluent reader: Oral reading strategies for building word recognition, fluency, and comprehension.* New York: Scholastic.

Tompkins, G.E. (2003). *Teaching writing: Balancing process and product* (4th ed.). Boston: Prentice Hall.

---

unteers to share their ideas "revoiced" by peers. A modification of this approach for ELLs could be to encourage students to partner-share their ideas, confusions, and questions in their native languages and then express them to the larger group by having the most proficient ELL translate into English the ideas, confusions, and questions. These ideas serve two important functions. First, they provide opportunities for students to be actively involved in the lesson. Second, because the students would have opportunities to make their thinking public, they would also provide the teacher with windows on their thinking. We focus on using these—and other means of assessment—to inform teachers' instructional practices in our discussion of the next principle.

Third Principle: Assessing Students' Understandings

Teachers should develop an ongoing plan for assessing ELLs' learning and modifying instruction based on students' learning needs.

Reflection Point 5.3

As you read Table 8, look at similarities and differences between the small-group activities and the whole-group lessons with respect to ongoing assessment, the focus of this principle. What do you consider to be your most significant observations ? Why?

Small-group interactions seemed to work best for Deng because he had immediate, and ongoing, opportunities to sort through confusions and develop new understandings and ideas about the text *Maniac Magee*. This is, perhaps, the single most powerful aspect of continual, authentic

Table 8
Assessing Understandings: Examples From Deng's Small Group and the Whole Class

Participation Structure	Key Events	Mrs. Weber's Actions	Beliefs Reflected in Mrs. Weber's Actions
Small-Group Activities	• As Deng engaged in small-group writing and discussion activities, his peers provided immediate commentary on his evolving understandings of *Maniac Magee*. • If Deng expressed confusion at any time, Tran and Chris tried to clarify his confusions.	• Earlier in the year, Mrs. Weber developed self-evaluation protocols for her students to use to assess their small-group behavior and that of their peers. • Across the year, Mrs. Weber provided instruction so that the students knew how to evaluate their participation in small groups.	• Students only learn to work effectively in small groups when the teacher models appropriate small-group behavior and students engage in on-going assessment to monitor their small-group participation. • The teacher must provide explicit instruction regarding literacy content, strategies, and skills prior to students working together in small groups.
Whole-Group Lessons	• Deng (and most of his classmates) only listened during whole-group lessons; therefore, there was no way for Mrs. Weber to assess their understandings of whole-group lessons.	• Mrs. Weber did not initiate any formal or informal assessment measures during whole-group instruction pertaining to *Maniac Magee*.	• What is taught will be learned. Thus, if students listen to instructional ideas they will understand them and assessments can take a summative, rather than formative, focus.

assessment that informs instruction—it can impact significantly students' learning in an immediate and ongoing manner (Au, Mason, & Scheu, 1995). A point worth noting from the examples in Table 8 (as well as our more extended discussions in chapters 3 and 4) is that the teacher is not the only one in a classroom who can assess on the spot and provide effective scaffolding of student learning (Chaiklin & Lave, 1996). Rather, as the example from chapter 4 of Tran and Chris helping Deng to understand racism illustrates, students can assess one another's understandings and provide guidance to one another in their learning. Thus, immediate and ongoing assessment can also occur when students assess themselves as well as one another. For example, Mrs. Weber taught her students to assess their participation in small groups and modify their behavior to improve their interactions in those groups. Opportunities for self-assessment pertaining to academic content and behavior are both important components of effective instructional practices.

Recent work by Cohen, Lotan, Abram, Scarloss, and Schultz (2002) on the potential effectiveness of small peer groups working together illustrates that powerful student learning can, indeed, occur in small groups given the right conditions. Studying small groups of sixth graders working on social studies projects, Cohen and her colleagues found that students did learn academic content through their small-group discussions as well as the work that they created together. "Moreover, learning was not a matter of relevant academic knowledge that individuals brought to the group but came about through reciprocal exchange of ideas and through a willingness to be self-critical about what the group was creating" (p. 1064). According to Cohen and her colleagues, the most effective learning occurred in small groups when students clearly understood the tasks they were being asked to complete and the criteria the teacher planned to use to evaluate their work. Teachers, they argue, play a central role in providing the necessary instruction to foster students' learning in small groups.

We are not suggesting—nor do we believe that Cohen and her colleagues are suggesting—that students' work together in small groups and their assessments of themselves and one another are sufficient in a teacher's overall instructional plan. However, as the case of Deng, Tran, and Chris talking about racism illustrates, successful peer interactions can promote students' learning. Designed and implemented effectively in classrooms, small-group work can be a powerful *addition* to a teacher's overall instructional plan. This is particularly the case when such work incorporates the teacher's day-to-day assessment to determine what students have understood as a result of their lessons and what they have yet to learn. Regular and ongoing teacher assessments—as well as individual and small-group assessments—can and should shape and inform a teacher's daily instruction. In Deng's case, if Mrs. Weber had mechanisms in place to check students' understanding in whole-group work, Deng would not have spent so many hours confused during these literacy lessons.

In the following chapter, we step back from, and out of, Deng's actual experiences and propose ideas for how the learning of ELLs might be facilitated more effectively in a different instructional context. We introduce you to Ms. Trost's classroom to illustrate how the three principles pertaining to ELLs that we have established in this chapter might be enacted through the activity settings Ms. Trost has created for her students, the nature of interactions she promotes within these settings, and the opportunities for authentic, ongoing assessment that are afforded in the ways she has organized her literacy instruction.

Book Club *Plus*: An Alternative Framework for Working With English-Language Learners

Walking into Elisabeth Trost's classroom, we see a set of words (pleaded, trembled) displayed by the overhead projector on a large screen in the front of the room. Students are working in small groups, their Book Clubs engaged in animated discussions, primarily in English, but with other languages occasionally heard (e.g., Spanish, Urdu). Ms. Trost's multicultural, multilingual students are reading the Newbery Medal–winning book Number the Stars *by Lois Lowry (1989). Their current task is to read the sentence from the book that contains a targeted word, then talk among themselves to draw inferences about what the word means in this context. Displayed on students' desks are their individual copies of the book, their reading logs, and, for Spanish-speaking students, a copy of the book in Spanish. The discussion of each word begins with one of the students reading the sentence in which the word appears to their peers in the group. The students use the similar spellings of* pleaded *and* please *as they make their initial inference about the meaning of the word* pleaded. *However, after a few students agree, one of the students suggests using more context clues, saying they should "find more words."*

> Gabriel: [reads sentence from book] "'I know I'm going to win the girl's race this week. I was second last week, but I've been practicing everyday. Come on, Ellen,' Annemarie pleaded," like if she was saying please.

79

Yeng: Yeah, that's what I think, too.

Leticia: If was she was saying please...

Araceli: We need to find more words.

The students agree and one of them decides to use the Spanish version to see if that might help them determine the meaning. Students shift briefly into Spanish at this point, indicating they found the sentence in that version of the text.

Araceli: I'm going to read it in Spanish.

Yesenia: I found it, Araceli.

Leticia: Ya lo encontré. [I found it.]

Araceli: Aquí está [Here it is], right here...

Several notice that key words have to do with the expression on Annemarie's face, leading to an exchange related to her emotional state, thus moving closer to the meaning of the target word.

Araceli: She was making like a face.

Thom: She was making a sad face.

Araceli: Yeah, a sad face...

Yesenia: I think always crying.

Leticia: Sad face.

Gabriel: I think always crying.

Yeng: Sad face.

Yesenia: Always crying...

Thom: No, I think it's going to be, um, always crying, because sad face is kinda the same thing.

Araceli: No, no because when you're sad [inaudible].

Thom: Then, if you cry your eyes [makes crying noises].

Ms. Trost's students actively work together to read the lines, read between the lines, and read beyond the lines as they focus on vocabulary that their teacher has targeted to help them understand *the story. The vocabulary building occurs through talk about text that engages all students in the classroom in active participation. Following students' time in peer-led discussions, they reconvene for a teacher-led session where each group presents their inferences about the word meanings, justifying them through the context clues they drew upon. For* pleaded, *groups have come up with "begging," "wanting something very badly," and "saying please to get what you want." Ms. Trost then asks students to act out the sentence, demonstrating in different ways what Annemarie would have sounded like if she were pleading (e.g., a whiny voice, a begging tone).*

Reflection Point 6.1 _____

Think about what you have observed through this window on Ms. Trost's lesson. What key elements for supporting ELL students' comprehension are visible in this segment? What role do the small-group discussions appear to play in students' meaning making? What role does native language appear to play in the students' vocabulary work in this setting?

___

aving presented background information in chapters 3, 4, and 5 about the instructional practices Deng experienced in his fifth-grade classroom, we now step back from our discussion of Deng's experiences and consider the following question: What instructional practices may better support ELLs' active participation in literacy learning? We address this question by exploring the instructional practices of a fourth-grade classroom in a Chicago elementary school serving a student population that is linguistically, culturally, and economically diverse. The teacher in this classroom, Ms. Trost, has extensive experience with students who are learning English and has adapted the Book Club *Plus* framework (Raphael, Florio-Ruane, George, Hasty, & Highfield, 2004) to meet the needs of her students' language and literacy learning. In this chapter, we describe Book Club *Plus* and recommend adaptations for teachers who have ELL students in their classrooms.

Our visit to Ms. Trost's classroom provides insights into how teachers can support and promote the learning of ELLs like Deng in mainstream classrooms. We wish to point out, however, that the ideas we present from Ms. Trost's classroom do not serve as a recipe for what to do with ELLs; rather, we present a problem-solving process in which Ms. Trost engaged that is unique to her particular teaching context. You may find the ideas that Ms. Trost developed useful as you sort out how to work effectively with the ELLs in your own unique context.

Next, we move away from a specific discussion of Ms. Trost's classroom practices to examine her ongoing journey learning to teach ELLs. Ms. Trost's professional development practices may inform your own thinking about ways you can continue to learn to meet the needs of the ELLs in your classroom. Finally, we come full-circle back to Deng, Taffy, and Cindy. We end this chapter, and the book, by discussing Deng's reflections on his learning as a result of working with us on this project. We also reflect on our own learning as a result of our work with Deng.

Stepping Back and Stepping Out: Introducing Ms. Trost

Over a dozen language groups are represented in Ms. Trost's fourth-grade classroom of 25 students who are learning English, with students at varying stages of confidence and competence in English language use. More than 70% of the students in Ms. Trost's school come from families classified as low income, based on the number of families who qualify for the U.S. federal free lunch program.

Ms. Trost is a member of the Book Club for English Language Learners Study Group associated with University of Illinois at Chicago. As a result of her interactions with other educators in her group, she has been learning about a literacy instructional framework called Book Club *Plus* and experimenting with it and modifying it for her ELLs. First, we describe Book Club *Plus* and provide examples of Ms. Trost's adaptations to this instructional framework for ELLs. We then describe how Ms. Trost incorporates the three principles of effective instruction (i.e., activities, interactions, and assessing understandings) introduced in chapter 5 for ELLs in her evolving literacy instructional practices.

Describing the Book Club *Plus* Instructional Framework

Taffy and several colleagues from the Teachers Learning Collaborative in southeast Michigan designed the original Book Club *Plus* instructional framework (Raphael et al., 2004). Interested in how this instructional framework might be used and adapted for students from diverse cultural, linguistic, and economic backgrounds in complex inner-city classrooms, Taffy and a small group of teachers from the Chicago metropolitan area formed a study group to explore ways to adapt the framework to teach English-language and literacy skills to students who were not native speakers of English. Ms. Trost was an instrumental founding member, who Taffy approached because of her reputation for teaching excellence in a multilingual setting. In turn, Ms. Trost was attracted to the idea of the study group because she felt that it would afford her the opportunity to engage in professional dialogue with colleagues about literacy instruction generally and, more specifically, the potential of Book Club *Plus* for supporting her ELL students' literacy learning.

The Book Club *Plus* curriculum framework helps teachers meet their dual commitments of (a) providing students with instruction using age-appropriate materials to encourage high levels of thinking through engaging and well-supported opportunities to read (or hear), write in response to, and talk about these texts and (b) providing students with activities designed to improve their basic reading skills with materials at their appropriate instructional levels.

The framework consists of two core contexts: Book Club and Literacy Block (see Raphael et al., 2004). (See Box 6.1 for Book Club resources.) The Book Club core context is organized around four activity settings: reading, writing, peer-led discussion, and whole-class minilessons and discussion (Raphael, Pardo, & Highfield, 2002). A central goal of Book Club is to help students develop a love for—and excitement about—literacy so that they will *want* to read and write. To support this focus, the books for the Book Club part of the instructional day have the potential to push students to consider big ideas or themes in their lives and the lives of others in the world. Examples in this chapter are from Ms. Trost's unit focusing on the overarching theme of "Courage in the Face of Challenges," using Lois Lowry's award-winning *Number the Stars* (1989) as the core novel. Ms. Trost promoted intertextual connections by relating the core text to thematically selected read-aloud books (e.g., *Butterfly* by Patricia Polacco [2000], *So Far From the Sea* by Eve Bunting [1998], *The Drinking Gourd* by F.N. Monjo [1993]), poetry and short essays from students' magazines, reference books such as *In Denmark It Could Not Happen* by H. Pundik (1998), as well as current events sources such as newspapers and magazines (e.g., *Time* or *Newsweek*).

The second core context for Book Club *Plus* is Literacy Block, organized around using texts to teach students at their appropriate instructional levels. Texts used can include leveled books, alternate levels of a basal reading program, and related literature written at a range of reading levels. As we will see in the sample lessons from Ms. Trost's ELL classroom, Literacy Block varies in the source materials used and the way it is put into practice. Perhaps the most common format involves three

---

Box 6.1
Book Club and Related Resources

Books

Cazden, C. (2001). *Classroom discourse: The language of teaching and learning.* Portsmouth, NH: Heinemann.

Gee, J.P. (1996). *Social linguistics and literacies: Ideology in discourses.* Bristol, PA: Taylor & Francis.

Raphael, T.E., Florio-Ruane, S., George, M., Hasty, N.L., & Highfield, K. (2004). *Book Club Plus! A literacy framework for the primary grades.* Lawrence, MA: Small Planet Communications.

Raphael, T.E., Kehus, M., & Damphousse, K. (2001). *Book Club for middle school.* Lawrence, MA: Small Planet Communications.

Raphael, T.E., Pardo, L.S., & Highfield, K. (2002). *Book Club: A literature-based curriculum* (2nd ed.). Lawrence, MA: Small Planet Communications.

Website

Planet Book Club

www.planetbookclub.com

guided reading groups composed of students working at, above, or below end-of-year grade-level expectations. The teacher alternates teaching the small groups, focusing on relevant skill and strategy instruction. When students are not with the teacher, they work independently, in pairs, or in small groups at learning centers (cf. Morrow, 2002), where they practice taught skills, work on unit- or theme-related projects, practice reading independently, and so forth. The learning center work is designed to support the instructional focuses of both the Book Club and guided reading activities. Yet such groupings may not be optimal for the necessary vocabulary growth ELLs need to perform on the same levels as their English-speaking peers. Ms. Trost's adaptations show how she has worked to meet her students' needs for literacy and language learning.

Ms. Trost's Adaptations to Book Club *Plus*

Ms. Trost instituted four adaptations to the typical Book Club *Plus* framework described above to support her students' language and literacy development: text selection, advance reading, extensive vocabulary work, and some grouping by native language. We describe each of these adaptations, in detail, in the context of a typical week of literacy instruction in Ms. Trost's classroom. Table 9 provides a window on the two-day cycle she repeats Monday through Thursday each week, with Friday providing flexibility for focusing on reading, writing, or a combination of the two.

The First Adaptation: Text Selection

When choosing her Book Club texts, Ms. Trost seeks native-language support wherever possible. Sometimes this can be done through already available commercial materials, most often for her Spanish-speaking students. For example, she was able to locate a Spanish-language book on tape for *Number the Stars* (*Quién Cuenta las Estrellas?* [Lowry, 1997]) in her unit on "Courage in the Face of Challenges." For another unit, "Exploring Families," using *Sarah, Plain and Tall* (MacLachlan, 1985), she was able to find a Spanish-language version, *Sarah, Sencilla y Alta* (MacLachlan, 1991). When native-language books or audiotapes were not already available, she was tenacious in (a) developing a community-based support

	Monday/Wednesday	Tuesday/Thursday	Friday
	Table 9		
	Overview of Ms. Trost's Literacy Instruction Cycle		
Homework	Students read the assigned chapter several times and start notes in reading log.	Students reread chapter, add to notes in reading log, and rewrite sentences where vocabulary words are found.	Varies depending on what students need based on the Monday–Thursday activities; begins with minilesson.
In Class	Literacy Block: Vocabulary work using Book Club core book Book Club: Read aloud text related to unit theme, followed by writing and talking about the text	Book Club: Students review chapter(s) read, write in reading logs, and discuss chapter in an extended community share, or group discussion, and in Book Clubs. Teacher reads aloud a related text, followed by an extended closing community share discussion. Students focus on • sharing reflections • asking questions • making connections • discussing theme	Book Club: Community Share Minilesson (e.g., comprehension strategies, writing strategies) in context of the unit core book and related read-aloud texts OR Writers Workshop: Opening Minilesson (e.g., writing strategy building on literature read) followed by Writers Workshop, contributing to development of unit theme

system by involving parents, family sponsors, older students, and others to record upcoming Book Club books in the languages that her students spoke and (b) inviting readers who spoke English in addition to the languages of the students in her classroom to read with her ELLs.

The Second Adaptation: Advance Reading

Before reading an assigned section of the book in class, students were instructed to read the section (e.g., a chapter) in advance of class, and

multiple times. As Ms. Trost knows, students in general become more fluent readers through repeated readings of a text (Worthy, Broaddus, & Ivey,
2001). She also knows that repeated readings are particularly important
for ELLs (García, 2003). Thus, from the beginning of the year, Ms. Trost set
up expectations that students would have done advance reading of the
assigned pages in their texts prior to the time they would discuss books
in small, peer-led groups. She opened the reading portion of her literacy
instruction every day by asking students to hold up the number of fingers
on their hand(s) to show how many times they had read the text—to a
family member, someone from the after-school program, someone in the
community, their resource or ELL/bilingual teacher, and so forth. Students
knew that Ms. Trost expected that it should take two hands (at least) to
show how many times they had read the pages.

The Third Adaptation: Extensive Vocabulary Work

After the students demonstrated that they had read the text several times,
Ms. Trost then turned to word study, the format for Literacy Block in her
classroom. For ELLs, a common and consistent source of text difficulty
is the text's vocabulary load. Thus, using leveled readers or even basal
textbooks from earlier grade levels would not address the language difficulties ELLs experience. To address this concern—because all of Ms.
Trost's students are ELLs—she devoted Literacy Block's guided reading
activities to word study. Ms. Trost developed a vocabulary instructional
framework that she calls VISELL (Vocabulary Instruction Support for
ELLs). She creates textbooks based on vocabulary from the novels students are reading during Book Club. She chooses three to five words for
each chapter or section of text that students are assigned to read during
the week, reproduces on paper and on overhead transparencies the paragraphs that contain these words, and uses these texts in vocabulary work
detailed in Table 10, her vocabulary instruction framework.

This format for Literacy Block draws on procedures that parallel the
work that Ms. Trost encouraged during Book Club. Notice that after students had a chance to locate and think about the words in the text on
their own, they then met in student-led groups to create their inferences
based on contextual information. Further, students were in mixed-
language groups in which they could draw on their background knowledge

---

Table 10
Ms. Trost's Vocabulary Instruction Support
for English-Language Learners (VISELL) Framework

1. On an overhead transparency, list three to five vocabulary words (or phrases) and the page numbers on which they appear.
2. Ask students to work independently to locate the word or phrase on page provided.
3. In groups of 4–6, students discuss what they "infer" the word to mean by reading it in context and sharing their inferences.
4. Each group constructs a new sentence, replacing the target word with the meaning, then rereading the sentence with their inferred meaning to determine whether their meaning makes sense.
5. Using choral response, ask students to say the word orally.
6. Students say the word.
7. Ask a student to read the paragraph containing the word.
8. Ask a student from each group to state the group's "inference" of the word's meaning.
9. Students replace the word with the inference and think aloud about whether it makes sense.
10. Record the conventional meaning on the transparency.
11. Ask students to create a sentence using the new word, and with sufficient context that someone reading their sentence could tell what the word meant or illustrate the word in a way that clearly conveys its meaning as used in the text.
12. Students create sentences in writing.
13. Students share sentences with a partner, and then several share with the whole group.

---

in their own language to discover words that share cognates (e.g., *situation* in English and *situación* in Spanish). The cognate chart posted on the wall was one reminder to students to always look for word similarities between their own language and English. Students moved from small groups to a whole-group discussion, parallel to community share, during which they took turns sharing their inferences. In that setting, Ms. Trost's role was to ensure that students had made appropriate inferences and to clarify any misunderstandings. It is crucial that students have extensive opportunities to sort out the meanings of the words—using text, each other as resources, and input from their teacher. Ms. Trost knows where input and guidance are needed because she has had opportunities to observe students in small-group interactions and to hear their questions and their contributions to the discussion of key concepts—as reflected through their vocabulary knowledge—from their text.

The Fourth Adaptation: Grouping by Native Language

Ms. Trost planned for, organized, and monitored the peer-led discussions, often grouping some of the student-led Books Clubs by native language. As much as she possibly could, Ms. Trost took into account her students' native languages, their confidence, and their willingness to take risks in speaking when establishing the Book Club group memberships. She finds that when students are able to use their native languages during peer-led discussions, they are more likely to stay on task.

Some Book Clubs were in English. Generally, English groups consist of students who have sufficient English to participate—like Deng in Mrs. Weber's room—and students who do not speak the same language as others in the class. Ms. Trost also set up native-language Book Club groups. For example, her Spanish group had one student who knew almost no English at all, one student with fairly good receptive English but not strong productive language skills (i.e., he understood far more than he could speak), and two speakers who were bilingual and biliterate. A similar group was arranged for Urdu-speaking students.

While the students talked in their peer-led discussion groups, Ms. Trost walked around the room to assess their understandings of the story as well as to monitor behavior. For students in the Spanish and Urdu groups, Ms. Trost paused the conversation and asked them to explain what they had been talking about. Students summarized in English—often by having the most fluent English speaker describe in English what others in the group were prompting him or her to tell their teacher. Thus, Ms. Trost's students knew it was important to be able to remember and articulate what they had talked about and why in their small-group discussions.

Typically, by the time students entered their Book Club discussion groups, they had read and reread the chapters for the day in one or more of the following ways: independently to family and community members, with a partner, as a recording at a listening center, with the resource teacher or an adult volunteer who knew their native language and English, and so forth. In this way, Ms. Trost ensured that her students had the scaffolding they needed to be able to know what the text was about. They also had extensive discussion of key concepts through the Literacy Block activities focused on vocabulary development; they heard their teacher read aloud several books that further developed the theme of their Book Club book; and they were part of a group of students who either shared their language or could support them in English. After their reading and prior to their discussion, all students wrote about the text they read or heard, recording in their reading logs the thoughts they had about the story (sometimes prompted, sometimes open-ended, or both). Remember that Ms. Trost allowed her students to write in English, in their native language, or in a combination of the two because she wanted to emphasize—in this context—deep thinking about the text. Thus, they were ready and able to participate in their peer-led discussion groups.

At the end of these peer-led discussions, students returned to the whole group for debriefing as they talked about what they thought the chapters were about and how the ideas in the chapters built on the theme of the unit, addressed questions raised in small groups, discussed challenging words they came across and could not define or use, and assessed their progress. Some of the discussion content was driven by the students' questions and comments, some by the teacher based on what she observed during the group discussion.

Ms. Trost's Instruction and the Three Principles for Instructing ELLs

The way that Ms. Trost structures her classroom and the nature of the activities within this structure reflect the following three principles that we introduced and discussed in chapter 5:

- Designing effective classroom activities
- Structuring effective interactions
- Assessing students' learning

Designing Effective Classroom Activities

First, Ms. Trost designs classroom activities within thematic units. Over the year each unit helps develop the yearlong focus—"Our Storied Lives"—that is characteristic of Book Club *Plus*. The creators of the framework use this overarching theme for both its pedagogical and its practical purposes. From a pedagogical level, students find units within this theme to be personally relevant and engaging (Raphael et al., 2002). Units within the overall theme build from "Stories of Self" to "Family Stories" to "Stories of Culture." Within the Stories of Self unit, students explore their own lives and how to represent their experiences using different genres. They read about the lives of others through narratives, poetry, song, and informational texts. This leads naturally to exploring Family Stories within the second unit since all individual stories are grounded by family experiences. Studying the various families and reading about other families leads naturally to the study of culture, since all families are grounded in cultural experiences. Thus, students are able to link the texts they read to their own lives—a feature that tends to engage students in the activities surrounding their reading as they move outward from self to eventually studying the world in which they live—crucial for both students with diverse linguistic, economic, and cultural backgrounds who are learning to understand one another and for relatively homogeneous students who need to learn to live and work in a diverse world with a global economy.

From a practical level, since literature—narrative as well as informational text—represents the recorded history of humanity (what we have learned, our values, our histories, and so forth), virtually any text can fit into one of these themes. Thus, Ms. Trost uses novels, such as *Number the Stars*, as a basis for a unit within "Stories of Culture" to explore broadly how people all over the world have had to have courage in the face of huge challenges. This theme is also used to connect students' own courageous experiences—many of them immigrants who had to leave behind friends, family, economic stability, and language in their move to the United States. She uses books like *Sarah, Plain and Tall* to introduce her students to important cultural knowledge about their new country (e.g., agrarian history, westward expansion, experiences of farmers and pioneers), while at the same time tapping into themes of displacement, (re)constructing families, and human interdependence. However, she finds other literature from a variety of genres and informational texts to expand on themes. For example, within the theme of courage, she also reads aloud poetry that conveys heroism, newspaper articles that describe heroic acts, and articles in children's magazines that describe how students have acted bravely. Also, books such as *So Far From the Sea* (Bunting, 1998) or *Faithful Elephants: A True Story of Animals, People and War* (Tsuchiya, 1988) provide ways for Ms. Trost to use read-alouds to extend the theme. The choice of Book Club *Plus*'s thematic organization opens the door for having all students read (or hear), write in response to, and talk about an age-appropriate text, while at the same time, the power of the theme provides Ms. Trost with a variety of text sources for teaching students at their instructional levels as well.

The thematic organization of Ms. Trost's units promotes intellectually challenging discussions and reflects high expectations for student literacy learning, but the instructional support is in place for students to succeed. Throughout the unit, students' ownership of literacy is encouraged as they explore themes and ideas important in their day-to-day lives, using literacy and language as tools for learning.

Structuring Effective Interactions

Ms. Trost's work with her students also reflects the second principle we introduced in chapter 5. She structures effective dialogic interactions in her classroom to promote her students' learning. For example, within the Book Club *Plus* setting, students talk with one another in same-language, small-group discussions; heterogeneous small-group discussions; teacher-led discussions; dyads; and other combinations. Students have opportunities to observe others in meaningful literacy activities, participating directly, as well as on the periphery, but in legitimate—in contrast to marginalized—ways (Lave & Wenger, 1991). For example, during the week of literacy instruction we described in Table 9 on p. 86, Ms. Trost held five peer-led discussion groups, including Spanish-language and Urdu-language Book Club groups and the vocabulary inference discussion groups. During peer-led discussion time, Ms. Trost visited each of the groups and took anecdotal notes to assess the students' understanding of the story. While visiting the Spanish and Urdu groups, she asked a student from the group to translate about the nature of the groups' discussions. This gave her a window on her students' understandings about the story in each of these groups.

Assessing Students' Learning

Within Book Club *Plus*, Ms. Trost engages in ongoing evaluation of students' reading, writing, and talk. In the previous section, we noted an example of how Ms. Trost assessed students' understandings during peer-led discussions. She also assesses students' understandings during other class-room contexts as well. For example, during whole-group lessons, Ms. Trost frequently uses think-pair-share, in which she asks her students to turn to a partner to answer a question or explain something about the focus of the ongoing lesson. Then she asks some students to share concerns, questions, confusions, and understandings that they are developing as they engage in the whole-group lesson. Additionally, Mr. Trost's students write on a regular basis. Ms. Trost reads her students' writing to get a sense of their evolving understandings. These, as well as other assessment practices, provide Ms. Trost with important information about when to step in and clarify misunderstandings so that, unlike Deng, her ELLs can make sense of the day-to-day lessons in a variety of instructional contexts.

Reflection Point 6.2_____

What do Ms. Trost's instructional practices reveal about her beliefs about literacy instruction for ELLs? What opportunities within your own classroom could you adapt to better meet the needs of ELLs?

Ms. Trost understands the lessons and activities in her classroom must be designed so that they are meaningful to the many ELLs in her classroom. Thus, she designed her thematic units to connect to the lives and experiences of her students. Also, she understands that employing a variety of participation structures (e.g., interactive whole group, small group, dyads) in her classroom is necessary to optimize the learning of her ELLs. She realizes that it is not enough to just place students in these different participation structures. She is familiar with the work of scholars such as Kris Gutiérrez (1992, 1994) that illustrates the importance of looking carefully at interactions within instructional frameworks to determine their usefulness for specific students in specific contexts. That is, adopting instructional frameworks alone is not sufficient. Teachers must attend carefully to the nature of the interactions that they foster within these frameworks.

The preceding comments relate to our third principle. Teachers and students must constantly monitor students' understandings in all classroom contexts. This is especially important for ELLs who may enter U.S. classrooms from culturally different schooling experiences. Scholars such as Delpit (1995) and de la Luz Reyes (1992) point out that teachers must monitor students' understandings and make explicit the classroom and cultural norms that ELLs may not be familiar with.

Ms. Trost as a Professional Educator

Not only does Ms. Trost understand the three principles about classroom instruction that we have discussed in this chapter; she has a complex understanding of human learning and a productive disposition about herself as a student of teaching. Particular *habits of mind* (Dewey, 1938) about learning—like the ones we introduced in chapters 1 and 2—are crucial when working with ELLs. That is, learning involves much more than rote memorization and applying low-level skills in particular academic domains like literacy. Learning involves understanding the rules and requirements (Gee, 2003) as well as developing deep understandings of important concepts and their relationships in these domains (Bransford, Brown, & Cocking, 2000). As an example of those points, recall the discussion of racism between Deng, Tran, and Chris. A low-level, discrete skills approach to trying to help Deng understand racism would be to have him look up the definition of racism in the dictionary, write it out, and memorize it for a Friday vocabulary test.

Such practices, in and of themselves, are not sufficient to help students understand the rules and requirements of particular academic domains, like literacy, or develop deep understandings of concepts. Scaffolded instruction—like the instruction that Ms. Trost provides in her classroom—in talking, reading, and writing about subjects such as racism in the context of meaningful discussions would, we argue, help students like Deng to develop deeper conceptual understandings of those subjects. As well, ELLs like Deng—actually, all learners for that matter—can only learn the rules and requirements for talking and writing about complex ideas presented in stories in the process of talking and writing about them in meaningful ways.

Not only does Ms. Trost see learning as a complex endeavor; she sees teaching this way, too. That is, she assumes the stance of an ethnographer in her teaching. We refer back to our discussion in chapters 1 and 2 to illustrate this point. As we demonstrated in chapter 2 with the vignette about Nick Jans (the teacher of Inupiat children in Alaska), when teachers assume an ethnographic stance in their work, they seek to understand the ways in which their students experience lessons and activities in their classrooms. They do this by listening to and watching students carefully as they engage in classroom lessons and activities, assuming competence on the part of their students, and suspending negative judgments while trying to understand why students act, talk, and write as they do.

Why does assuming an ethnographic stance matter in our work with ELLs? Ms. Trost understands that different cultural and linguistic backgrounds influence the ways in which students experience school (Valdés, 2001). If students experience classroom lessons and activities in different ways, what constitutes "good" teaching will vary depending on students' experiences and needs (Gay, 2000). Remember the example we presented in chapter 2 about the teachers in the rural Oregon town where a significant shift in student population occurred across a 20- to 30-year period. What may have constituted good teaching at one period of time with a particular group of European American students was not good teaching 25 years later when the student population shifted to include significant numbers of Latino and Native American students from different linguistic and cultural backgrounds. Ms. Trost recognizes that there is no such thing as a universal form of "good teaching" (Gay, 2000). Rather, to be "good" teaching, the practices must fit the specific students and their needs within the particular contexts of instruction (Gutiérrez, 1992, 1994). That is, Ms. Trost did not look for a checklist of characteristics about particular groups to apply in her teaching. This simplistic practice—all too common in educational settings—does not take into account the complexities within and across cultural groups (Ferdman, 1990). As the case of Deng's learning illustrated, what worked in the whole-group lessons for European American students did not work for Deng.

It could be argued that Ms. Trost assumed more of an ethnographic stance toward her ELLs than did Mrs. Weber. However, because all of Ms. Trost's students were ELLs, her teaching context certainly made the need to assume this stance more evident. While Mrs. Weber had a culturally and linguistically diverse class, all of her students—except for Deng—were proficient in English. Since more U.S. teachers teach in contexts similar to Mrs. Weber's classroom (Howard, 1999), it more critical than ever that all mainstream teachers—even if they only have a few ELLs—understand the extent to which their oftentimes silent ELLs may be experiencing serious confusion during classroom lessons and activities. If Mrs. Weber had been aware of the extent to which Deng was confused in whole-group lessons, she undoubtedly would have made significant changes to her instruction.

Finally, Ms. Trost is aware that what she knows and understands now is not a sufficient knowledge base for the remainder of her career as a teacher. Ms. Trost sees herself as a lifelong learner. As a teacher of literacy, Ms. Trost knows that she must be a reader and writer herself (Jacobs & Tunnell, 2004). She subscribes to, and reads, key literacy journals that give her ideas for her own teaching of literacy, in general, and her work with ELLs, in particular. In addition to subscribing to key journals, Ms. Trost also belongs to professional organizations, and she attends state and national conferences of these organizations whenever possible. (For a list of professional associations, see Box 6.2.)

Ms. Trost also has developed a professional library that includes many books about literacy instruction, in general, and literacy instruction for ELLs, in particular. While reading professional literature is a must for teachers as individuals, Ms. Trost also knows that when teachers work together as communities of readers and writers, learning can be more powerful and more fun. When teachers meet with others they can share ideas and practices and problem solve together about what worked in their classrooms and what did not and why. As we mentioned earlier in this chapter, Ms. Trost is a member of a professional teacher–learner collaborative called the Book Club for English-Language Learners Study Group. Teachers in Ms. Trost's group meet on a regular basis to read professional literature, reflect on their classroom practices, and sort out thorny problems of practice in their teaching. In addition to membership in informal study groups, Ms. Trost has continued her professional development in other ways—earning her bilingual certification in the state of Illinois.

Finally, in addition to all of the important ways Ms. Trost engages in professional development to meet the needs of her ELLs, there are other

---

Box 6.2
Professional Associations

Center for Applied Linguistics
www.cal.org

Center for the Improvement of Early Reading Achievement (CIERA)
www.ciera.org

International Reading Association (IRA)
www.reading.org

National Association for Bilingual Education (NABE)
www.nabe.org

National Council of Teachers of English (NCTE)
www.ncte.org

National Education Association
www.nea.org

National Reading Conference
www.nronline.org

New Teacher Center at UC Santa Cruz
www.newteachercenter.org

Phonological Awareness Literacy Screening (PALS)/Nevada
http://literacy.ddig.com/Nevada

PALS/University of Virginia
http://curry.edschool.virginia.edu/curry/centers/pals/home.html

Teachers of English to Speakers of Other Languages (TESOL)
www.tesol.org

---

ideas you might consider. For example, you can write grants requests to acquire books and materials in multiple languages for your classroom and school or to invite authors and scholars from diverse cultural and linguistic backgrounds to provide meaningful inservices to the students and teachers at your school. (See the websites for IRA and NCTE in Box 6.2 for examples of organizations to which grants can be written.) Some of our colleagues in public schools have developed extensive libraries of leveled sets of books for teachers to check out. We suggest that the selection you acquire for your school and classrooms include books written in a host of different languages as well as many culturally relevant texts. (See Box 6.3 for a suggested list of multicultural children's literature.)

Box 6.3
Multicultural Literature for Children

African American Children's Books

Middle Grades

Hamilton, V. (1967). *Zeely*. New York: Macmillan.

Hamilton, V. (1995). *Her stories: African-American folk tales, fairy tales, and true tales*. New York: Scholastic.

Parks, R. (with Reed, G.J.). (1996). *Dear Mrs. Parks*. New York: Lee & Low Books.

Intermediate/Young Adult

Berry, J. (1987). *A thief in the village*. New York: Orchard.

Berry, J. (1993). *Ajeemah and his son*. New York: Orchard.

Cox, C. (1991). *Undying glory: The story of the Massachusetts 54th Regiment*. New York: Scholastic.

Stowe, H. (1988). *Uncle Tom's cabin*. New York: Signet Classic.

Taylor, M. (1991). *Let the circle be unbroken*. New York: Puffin.

Taylor, M. (1997). *Roll of thunder, hear my cry*. New York: Puffin.

Asian Pacific American Children's Books

Elementary Grades

Brown, J.M. (1994). *Thanksgiving at Obaachan's*. Chicago: Polychrome.

Chin-Lee, C. (1993). *Almond cookies and dragon well tea*. Chicago: Polychrome.

Sakai, K. (1990). *Sachiko means happiness*. Emeryville, CA: Children's Book Press.

Sook, N.C. (1993). *Halmoni and the picnic*. Boston: Houghton Mifflin.

Middle Grades

Garland, S. (1993). *The lotus seed*. New York: Harcourt.

Hosozawa-Nagano, E. (1995). *Chopsticks from America*. Chicago: Polychrome.

Uchida, Y. (1972). *Samurai of the gold hill*. New York: Scribner.

Uchida, Y. (1981). *A jar of dreams*. New York: Atheneum.

Uchida, Y. (1993). *The bracelet*. New York: Philomel.

Intermediate/Young Adult

Crew, L. (1989). *Children of the river*. New York: Delacorte.

Lee, M.G. (1992). *Finding my voice*. Boston: Houghton Mifflin.

Sook, N.C. (1994). *Gathering of pearls*. Boston: Houghton Mifflin.

(continued)

Box 6.3
Multicultural Literature for Children (continued)

Latino and Hispanic American Children's Books
Elementary Grades

Delacre, L. (1989). *Arroz con leche: Popular songs and rhymes from Latin America*. New York: Scholastic.

Belpre, P. (1991). *Perez and Martina: A Puerto Rican folktale*. New York: Viking Penguin.

Mike, J. (1995). *Juan Bobo and the horse of seven colors: A Puerto Rican legend*. New York: Troll Communications.

Mora, P. (1994). *The desert is my mother/El desierto es mi madre*. Houston: Piñata/Arte Publico.

Ober, H. (1994). *How music came to the world: An ancient Mexican myth*. Boston: Houghton Mifflin.

Rice, J. (1993). *La nochebuena south of the border*. Gretna, LA: Pelican.

Middle Grades

Ada, A.F. (1993). *My name is Maria Isabel*. Ill. K. Dyble Thompson. New York: Atheneum.

Crespo, G. (1993). *How the sea began: A Taino myth*. New York: Clarion.

Marinez, E.C. (1995). *Coming to America: The Mexican American experience*. Brookfield, CT: Millbrook Press.

Mohr, N. (1979). *Felita*. New York: Dial Press.

Intermediate/Young Adult

Lankford, M.D. (1994). *Quinceañera: A Latina's journey to womanhood*. Brookfield, CT: Millbrook Press.

Mohr, N. (1986). *Going home*. New York: Dial Press.

Native American Children's Books
Elementary Grades

Ahenakew, F. (1988). *How the birch tree got its stripes*. Saskatoon, Saskatchewan, Canada: Fifth House.

Jones, H. (1971). *The trees stand shining: Poetry of North American Indians*. New York: Dial Books.

Sneve, V.D.H. (1989). *Dancing teepees*. New York: Holiday House.

Wheeler, B. (1986). *Where did you get your moccasins?* Winnipeg, Manitoba, Canada: Pemmican Publications.

Middle Grades

Ancona, G. (1993). *Powwow*. San Diego: Harcourt Brace Jovanovich.

Culleton, B. (1986). *Spirit of the white bison*. Winnipeg, Manitoba, Canada: Pemmican Publications.

Lacapa, M. (1992). *Antelope woman*. Flagstaff, AZ: Northland Publishing.

Sneve, V.D.H. (1994). *The Seminoles*. New York: Holiday House.

Swentzell, R. (1992). *Children of clay: A family of Pueblo potters*. Minneapolis, MN: Lerner.

Turcotte, M. (1995). *Songs of our ancestors: Poems about Native Americans*. Chicago: Children's Book Press.

Yamane, L. (1994). *When the world ended...and other Rumsien Ohlone stories*. Berkeley, CA: Oyate.

Intermediate/Young Adult

Walters, A.L. (1993). *Neon pow-wow: New Native American voices of the Southwest*. Flagstaff, AZ: Northland Publishing.

Coming Full Circle: Thinking About Deng's Learning and Our Own

Drawing on Harvey Graff, Gee (1990) argues that popular conceptions of literacy imbue those who are literate (i.e., those who can read and write) with almost limitless power. For example, the ability to read and write influences and determines individuals' productivity, wealth, ability to maintain and preserve a democracy, and so forth. Graff calls this popular conception of the powerful effects of literacy "the literacy myth" (as cited in Gee, 1990, p. 32). Gee argues convincingly that

> contrary to the literacy myth, *nothing* follows from literacy or schooling. Much follows, however, from what comes *with* literacy and schooling, what literacy and schooling come wrapped up in, namely the attitudes, values, norms and beliefs (at once social, cultural & political) that always accompany literacy and schooling. (p. 42, emphasis in original)

It is not literacy per se, but the practices associated with being enculturated into the use of spoken, written, and enacted language in particular ways, that shapes individuals' abilities to choose various ways of being in society. It follows, then, that educators ought not to conceive of literacy as a set of discrete skills to memorize and master. Rather, in our classrooms, we must attend carefully to the oftentimes tacit ways that we teach our students to use reading, writing, and speaking. This point is particularly salient when working with ELLs. In order to function in the circles of economic, political, and social power in this country, individuals must understand the attitudes, values, norms, and beliefs with which language is used in those spheres of influence. And these attitudes, values, norms, and beliefs are taught and learned in and through social interactions.

Gee's (2003) conception of literacy parallels our conception of opportunity. That is, opportunities are created between individuals through particular types of interactions in specific contexts. Like literacy, learning opportunities are completely social. Those who perpetuate the common conception that America is the land of opportunity and anyone who works hard enough can achieve financial and social success place the onus of responsibility for succeeding squarely on the shoulders of the individual. By spotlighting the individual, the functioning of social institutions, such as schools, often goes unexamined or underexamined. If the power of literacy learning opportunities exists in social practices, and social institutions such as schools are one of the primary institutions where these practices are taught and learned, it is imperative that we attend critically to the structure of the institutions and the nature of the social practices that occur there.

By working with us as an informant about his own literacy learning, Deng was socialized into a particular way of using language and envisioning his own future educational plans and opportunities. For example, through our interactions he learned to articulate and justify his beliefs about his own learning experiences. He learned about the value of his native language as we used both Hmong and English to discern his conceptions of his literacy learning (Brock, 1997). He learned, too, that his thoughts and ideas can count as very important to others, and he demonstrated an understanding of the importance of documenting this thinking and learning. (For example, he mentioned one time that he'd be happy to read aloud *Maniac Magee* [Spinelli, 1990] into a tape recorder and do a think-aloud about his understanding of the story as he read if we would provide him with a tape recorder and blank tapes.) Moreover, he learned about the importance of college (although it did not seem quite clear to him why anyone—like Taffy and Cindy—would keep going to school until the 22nd grade) and that writing is an important venue in our educational system to express the thinking and learning that occur as we study teaching and learning.

On several occasions, after our research project was completed, Deng made reference to his future plans to go to college and write a dissertation of his own. One Saturday, Deng and his two younger sisters went to Cindy's house so that they could use her computer to work on school projects (a report on Nebraska and a diorama about the Inupiat Indians). During their time together that morning, Cindy showed Deng a draft of a conference paper that she was writing about their research together, her boxes of tapes and notebooks, and a copy of a friend's completed dissertation so that he could see a finished document. After working with Deng that day, Cindy wrote the following:

> As we were talking he [Deng] said that he wanted to get his Ph.D. too
> when he gets older. We have talked about this in the past. Today, he told

> me that the only problem with getting his Ph.D. is that he isn't sure what
> he will write his dissertation about. I told him that this isn't something he
> has to worry about right now—that there will be plenty of time for him
> to think about that as he gets older! (Field notes, March 23)

Shortly before the end of Deng's sixth-grade school year, his mother re-married and his family moved to North Carolina. Cindy received a letter from Deng that summer. In that letter, Deng told her of his plans to go to college: "CINDY WHEN I GOING TO COLLEGE I WILL GO TO MICHIGAN STATE UNIVERSITY" (Letter from Deng, capitals in original).

Our learning experiences together are now a part of Deng's history. However, this collaborative experience studying Deng's literacy learning with him—as well as countless others in and out of school—has the potential to affect Deng's future positively. Deng will have a hand in shaping his own future educational opportunities; however, the influence of those experiences and opportunities will also be shaped by the teachers and peers Deng encounters as he continues his journey through the U.S. educational system.

Whether Deng continues to see college and a PhD as a viable alternative in his life will depend partly on the remainder of his learning experiences as he completes middle school and high school. Thus, Deng's future learning opportunities are not solely in his hands: To a great extent, they will be shaped by the nature of his interactions within and across various social institutions (e.g., home, school, and community). With respect to the classrooms and broader educational systems within which he will participate, our hope is that his current and future teachers recognize and take seriously their awesome responsibility to help socialize Deng, as well as other ELLs like him, into the literacy practices that will enable him to have the choice to participate in social, economic, and political circles of influence in the United States. We believe that the small-group interactions we highlighted in Mrs. Weber's classroom and the many different participation structures we highlighted in Ms. Trost's classroom will help ELLs, like Deng, understand the literacy practices necessary to engage successfully in U.S. society at any level they choose.

We have talked a bit about how Deng was influenced by our work together; we suspect, however, that Deng's work with us has influenced us and transformed our thinking and learning much more than we influenced his. Our friend and colleague Susan Florio-Ruane suggests that in educational encounters, it is often the student who is expected to change, grow, and learn (2002). She admonishes us, as educators, to embrace "the possibility of transformation by means of engagement" with our students (p. 29). When asked to name our most powerful and influential teachers, Deng is one person we place at the top of our respective lists. We believe that we have been transformed by our engagement with Deng in this project, and we thank him for his willingness to be our teacher.

References

Au, K.H. (1993). *Literacy instruction in multicultural settings*. Fort Worth, TX: Holt, Rinehart & Winston.

Au, K.H., Mason, J.M., & Scheu, J.A. (1995). *Literacy instruction for today*. New York: HarperCollins College.

August, D., & Hakuta, K. (Eds.). (1997). *Improving schooling for language-minority children: A research agenda*. Washington, DC: National Academy Press.

Berliner, D.C., & Biddle, B.J. (1995). *The manufactured crisis: Myths, fraud, and the attack on America's public schools*. Menlo Park, CA: Addison-Wesley.

Bransford, J.D., Brown, A.L., & Cocking, R.R. (Eds.). (2000). *How people learn: Brain, mind, experience, and school*. Washington, DC: National Academy Press.

Brock, C.H. (1997). *Exploring a second language learner's opportunities for literacy learning in a mainstream classroom: A collaborative case study analysis*. Unpublished doctoral dissertation, Michigan State University, East Lansing, Michigan.

Brock, C.H. (2001). Working with English language learners in English dominant classrooms: Considerations from research and practice. *Language Arts*, *78*(5), 467–475.

Brock, C.H., Boyd, F.B., & Moore, J. (2003). Variation in language and the use of language across contexts: Implications for literacy learning. In J. Flood, D. Lapp, J.R. Squire, & J.M. Jensen (Eds.), *Handbook of research on teaching the English language arts* (2nd ed., pp. 446–458). Mahwah, NJ: Erlbaum.

Brock, C.H., McVee, M.B., Shojgreen-Downer, A., & Flores-Dueñas, L. (1998). No habla inglés: Critically exploring the construction of an English language learner's access to classroom discourse in a predominantly English-speaking classroom. *The Bilingual Research Journal*, *22*(2, 3, & 4), 175–200.

Brock, C.H., Moore, D., & Parks, L. (2003). *Critically analyzing the process of preparing preservice teachers to teach in culturally and linguistically diverse classrooms*. Paper presented at the National Reading Conference, Scottsdale, AZ.

Brock, C.H., & Raphael, T.E. (1994). Envisionment building: A second-language student constructing meaning during a social studies unit. In C.K. Kinzer &

D.J. Leu (Eds.), *43rd yearbook of the National Reading Conference* (pp. 89–100). Chicago: National Reading Conference.

Brock, C.H., & Raphael, T.E. (2003). Teaching children to become insiders: Guiding children to appropriate a new written discourse. *The Elementary School Journal, 103*(5), 481–502.

Cazden, C. (1988). *Classroom discourse: The language of teaching and learning.* Portsmouth, NH: Heinemann.

Chaiklin, S., & Lave, J. (1996). *Understanding practice: Perspectives on activity and context.* New York: Cambridge University Press.

Chan, S. (1994). *Hmong means free: Life in Laos and America.* Philadelphia: Temple University Press.

Cohen, E.G., Lotan, R.A., Abram, P.L., Scarloss, B.A., & Schultz, S.E. (2002). Can groups learn? *Teachers College Record, 104*(6), 1045–1068.

Covey, S.R. (1989). *The seven habits of highly effective people: Powerful lessons in personal change.* New York: Simon & Schuster.

Crawford, J. (1995). *Bilingual education: History, politics, theory, and practice* (3rd ed.). Los Angeles: Bilingual Educational Services.

Cummins, J. (1994). Knowledge, power, and identity in teaching English as a second language. In F. Genesee (Ed.), *Educating second language children: The whole child, the whole curriculum, the whole community* (pp. 33–58). New York: Cambridge University Press.

Cummins, J. (2001). *Language, power, and pedagogy: Bilingual children in the crossfire.* Buffalo, NY: Multilingual Matters.

de la Luz Reyes, M. (1992). Challenging venerable assumptions: Literacy instruction for linguistically different students. *Harvard Educational Review, 62,* 427–447.

Delpit, L. (1995). *Other people's children: Cultural conflict in the classroom.* New York: The New Press.

Dewey, J. (1938). *Experience and education.* New York: Collier Books.

Diller, D. (2003). Learning to look through a new lens: One teacher's reflection on the change process as related to cultural awareness. In F.B. Boyd, C.H. Brock, & M.S. Rozendal (Eds.), *Multicultural and multilingual literacy and language practices: Constructing contexts for empowerment.* New York: Guilford.

Eisner, E. (1998). *The enlightened eye: Qualitative inquiry and the enhancement of educational practice.* Columbus, OH: Prentice Hall.

Erickson, F., & Shultz, J. (1992). Students' experience of the curriculum. In P.W. Jackson (Ed.), *Handbook of research on curriculum* (pp. 465–485). New York: Macmillan.

Ferdman, B.M. (1990). Literacy and cultural identity. *Harvard Educational Review, 60*(2), 181–203.

Florio-Ruane, S. (2002). *Teacher education and the cultural imagination.* Mahwah, NJ: Erlbaum.

Frank, C. (1999). *Ethnographic eyes: A teacher's guide to classroom observation.* Portsmouth, NH: Heinemann.

Freeman, Y.S., & Freeman, D.E. (with Mercuri, S.). (2002). *Closing the achievement gap: How to reach limited-formal-schooling and long-term English learners*. Portsmouth, NH: Heinemann.

Garcia, E.E. (1990). Educating teachers for language minority students. In W.R. Houston, M. Haberman, & J. Sikula (Eds.), *Handbook of research on teacher education* (pp. 717–729). New York: Macmillan.

García, G.G. (Ed.). (2003). *English learners: Reaching the highest level of English literacy*. Newark, DE: International Reading Association.

Garrison, J. (1995). Deweyan pragmatism and the epistemology of contemporary social constructivism. *American Educational Research Journal, 32*(4), 716–740.

Gay, G. (2000). *Culturally responsive teaching: Theory, research, and practice*. New York: Teachers College Press.

Gee, J.P. (1990). *Social linguistics and literacies: Ideology in discourses*. London: Falmer Press.

Gee, J.P. (1996). *Social linguistics and literacies: Ideology in discourses* (2nd ed.). London: Falmer Press.

Gee, J.P. (2003). Opportunity to learn: A language-based perspective on assessment. *Assessment in Education, 10*(1), 27–46.

Geertz, C. (1973). *The interpretation of cultures*. New York: Basic Books.

George, M., Raphael, T.E., & Florio-Ruane, S. (2003). Connecting children, culture, curriculum, and text. In G.G. García (Ed.), *English learners: Reaching the highest level of English literacy* (pp. 308–332). Newark, DE: International Reading Association.

Gill, J. (1993). *Learning to learn: Toward a philosophy of education*. Atlantic Highlands, NJ: Humanities Press.

Goatley, V.J., Brock, C.H., & Raphael, T.E. (1995). Diverse learners participating in regular education "book clubs." *Reading Research Quarterly, 30*(3), 352–380.

Gutiérrez, K. (1992). A comparison of instructional contexts in writing process classrooms with Latino children. *Education and Urban Society, 24*, 244–262.

Gutiérrez, K. (1994). How talk, context and script share contexts for learning: A cross-case comparison of journal sharing. *Linguistics and Education, 5*, 335–365.

Hamilton-Merritt, J. (1993). *Tragic mountains: The Hmong, the Americans, and the secret wars for Laos, 1942–1992*. Indianapolis: Indiana University Press.

Howard, G. (1999). *We can't teach what we don't know: White teachers, multiracial schools*. New York: Teachers College Press.

Hudelson, S., Poynor, L., & Wolfe, P. (2003). Teaching bilingual and ESL children and adolescents. In J. Flood, D. Lapp, J.R. Squire, & J.M. Jensen (Eds.), *Handbook of research on teaching the English language arts* (2nd ed., pp. 421–434). Mahwah, NJ: Erlbaum.

Jacob, E., & Jordan, C. (Eds.). (1993). *Minority education: Anthropological perspectives*. Norwood, NJ: Ablex.

Jacobs, J.S., & Tunnell, M.O. (2004). *Children's literature, briefly*. Columbus, OH: Pearson Merrill Prentice Hall.

Jans, N. (1993). *Last light breaking: Living among Alaska's Inupiat Eskimos*. Portland, OR: Alaska Northwest Books.

Krashen, S.D. (2003). *Explorations in language acquisition and use*. Portsmouth, NH: Heinemann.

Ladson-Billings, G. (1994). *The dreamkeepers: Successful teachers of African-American children*. San Francisco: Jossey-Bass.

Langer, J. (1984). Examining background knowledge and text comprehension. *Reading Research Quarterly, 19*(4), 468–491.

Lave, J. (1996). Teaching, as learning, in practice. *Mind, Culture, and Activity, 3*(3), 149–164.

Lave, J., & Wenger, E. (1991). *Situated learning: Legitimate peripheral participation*. New York: Cambridge University Press.

Major, E., & Brock, C.H. (2003). Fostering appropriate dispositions towards diverse learners amongst teacher candidates: Sorting through a moral dilemma. *Teacher Education Quarterly, 30*(4), 7–27.

McMahon, S., & Raphael, T.E. (with Goatley, V.J., & Pardo, L.S.). (1997). *The Book Club connection: Literacy learning and classroom talk*. New York: Teachers College Press.

Morrow, L.M. (2002). *The literacy center: Contexts for reading and writing*. Portland, ME: Stenhouse.

National Clearinghouse for English Language Acquisition & Language Instruction Educational Programs. (2002). *English language learners & the U.S. Census, 1990–2000*. Retrieved from http://www.ncela.gwu.edu/policy/states/ellcensus 90s.pdf

Nieto, S. (1999). *The light in their eyes: Creating multicultural learning communities*. New York: Teachers College Press.

Oaks, E. (1985). *Keeping track: How schools structure inequality*. New Haven, CT: Yale University Press.

Paratore, J.R., & McCormack, R.L. (Eds.). (1997). *Peer talk in the classroom: Learning from research*. Newark, DE: International Reading Association.

Paterson, K. (1981). *Gates of excellence: On reading and writing books for children*. New York: Dutton Juvenile.

Pearson, P.D. (1997). Commentary: Extending research on the Book Club program. In S. McMahon & T.E. Raphael (Eds.), *The Book Club connection: Literacy learning and classroom talk* (pp. 222–223). New York: Teachers College Press.

Raphael, T.E., & Brock, C.H. (1993). Mei: Learning the literacy culture in an urban elementary school. In C.K. Kinzer & D.J. Leu (Eds.), *42nd yearbook of the National Reading Conference* (pp. 179–189). Chicago: National Reading Conference.

Raphael, T.E., Florio-Ruane, S., George, M., Hasty, N.L., & Highfield, K. (2004). *Book Club* Plus! *A literacy framework for the primary grades*. Lawrence, MA: Small Planet Communications.

Raphael, T.E., Pardo, L.S., & Highfield, K. (2002). *Book Club: A literature-based curriculum* (2nd ed.). Lawrence, MA: Small Planet Communications.

Rodriguez, R. (1989). *Hunger of memory: The education of Richard Rodriguez*. New York: Bantam Books.

Rose, M. (1989). *Lives on the boundary: A moving account of the struggles and achievements of America's educationally underprepared*. New York: Penguin Books.

Schecter, S.R., & Cummins, J. (Eds.). (2003). *Multilingual education in practice: Using diversity as a resource*. Portsmouth, NH: Heinemann.

Spindler, G., & Spindler, L. (2000). *Fifty years of anthropology and education 1950–2000: A Spindler anthology* (G. Spindler, Ed.). Mahwah, NJ: Erlbaum.

Tharp, R. (1997). *From at-risk to excellence: Research, theory and principles for practice*. Santa Cruz, CA: Center for Research on Education, Diversity, & Excellence.

Thomas, W.P., & Collier, V.P. (2001). *A national study of school effectiveness for language minority students' long-term academic achievement*. Report prepared with funding from the Center for Research on Education, Diversity & Excellence (CREDE), a national research center funded by the Office of Educational Research and Improvement (OERI) of the U.S. Department of Education, under Cooperative Agreement No. R306A60001-96 (July 1, 1996–June 30, 2001).

Tompkins, G.E. (2001). *Literacy for the 21st century: A balanced approach* (2nd ed.). New York: Merrill Prentice Hall.

Valdés, G. (2001). *Learning and not learning English: Latino students in American schools*. New York: Teachers College Press.

Valenzuela, A. (1999). *Subtractive schooling*. Albany: State University of New York Press.

Walker-Moffat, W. (1995). *The other side of the Asian American success story*. San Francisco: Jossey-Bass.

Wells, G. (1999). *Dialogic inquiry: Toward a sociocultural practice and theory of education*. New York: Cambridge University Press.

Wolcott, H.F. (2001). *Ethnography: A way of seeing*. Walnut Creek, CA: Altamira Press.

Wong Fillmore, L., & Snow, C. (2002). What teachers need to know about language. In C. Temple Adger, C. Snow, & D. Christian (Eds.), *What teachers need to know about language* (pp. 7–54). McHenry, IL: Center for Applied Linguistics & Delta Systems.

Worthy, J., Broaddus, K., & Ivey, G. (2001). *Pathways to independence: Reading, writing, and learning in grades 3–8*. New York: Guilford.

Children's Literature References

Bunting, E. (1998). *So far from the sea*. New York: Houghton Mifflin.

Lowry, L. (1989). *Number the stars*. New York: Houghton Mifflin.

Lowry, L. (1997). *Quién cuenta las estrellas?* (J. Luque, Trans.). Madrid: Espasa Calpe Mexicana.

MacLachlan, P. (1985). *Sarah, plain and tall*. New York: HarperCollins.

MacLachlan, P. (1991). *Sarah, sencilla y alta* (M. Sansigre, Trans.). Lyndhurst, NJ: Lectorum.

Monjo, F.N. (1993). *The drinking gourd: A story of the underground railroad*. New York: HarperCollins. (Original work published 1970)

Polacco, P. (2000). *Butterfly*. New York: Philomel.

Pundik, H. (1998). *In Denmark it could not happen: The flight of the Jews to Sweden in 1943*. New York: Gefen Publishing House.

Spinelli, J. (1990). *Maniac Magee*. New York: Harper.

Tsuchiya, Y. (1988). *Faithful elephants: A true story of animals, people and war*. Boston: Houghton Mifflin.

Index

Note: Page references followed by *b*, *f*, or *t* indicate boxes, figures, or tables, respectively.

A

ABRAM, P.L., 77
ACTIVE LEARNING: elements of, 74
ADA, A.F., 73*b*, 99*b*
ADVANCE READING: in Book Club *Plus*, 86–87
AFRICAN AMERICANS: children's books on, 98*b*
AHENAKEW, F., 99*b*
ALMASI, J., 54*b*
ANCONA, G., 99*b*
ASIAN PACIFIC AMERICANS: children's books on, 98*b*
ASSESSMENT: in Book Club *Plus*, 92–94; of student understandings, 75–78, 76*t*
AU, K.H., 29, 75*b*, 77
AUGUST, D., 4

B

BALLENTINE, D., 49*b*
BASIC INTERPERSONAL COMMUNICATION SKILLS (BICS), 23
BELPRE, P., 99*b*
BERLINER, D.C., 30
BERRY, J., 98*b*
BICS. *See* basic interpersonal communication skills
BIDDLE, B.J., 30
BILINGUAL EDUCATION, 22; resources on, 23*b*
BOOK CLUB, 83–84; resources for, 84*b*
BOOK CLUB *PLUS*, 79–103; adaptations to, 85–90; assessment in, 92–94; instructional framework of, 83–85; literacy instruction cycle in, 86*t*; yearlong focus in, 90
BOYD, F., 73*b*
BOYLE, O.F., 73*b*
BRANSFORD, J.D., 94
BROADDUS, K., 87
BROCK, C.H., 4–5, 26, 34–35, 39, 48, 73*b*, 101

BROWN, A.L., 94
BROWN, J.M., 98*b*
BUNTING, E., 84, 91

C

CAI, M., 49*b*
CALP. *See* cognitive academic language proficiency
CARROLL, J., 75*b*
CARY, S., 26*b*
CASEY, M., 6*b*
CAZDEN, C., 42, 68, 84*b*
CHAIKLIN, S., 77
CHAN, S., 10
CHARACTER MAP, 55–56, 55*t*, 56*f*
CHIN-LEE, C., 98*b*
CLASSROOM ACTIVITIES: for ELL instruction, 90–92; structuring, 69–71, 70*t*
COCKING, R.R., 94
COGNITIVE ACADEMIC LANGUAGE PROFICIENCY (CALP), 23
COHEN, E.G., 54*b*, 77
COLLIER, V.P., 1, 19, 21–22, 24
CONNELLY, M., 23*b*
CONTINUING EDUCATION: teachers and, 96
COVEY, S.R., 25, 31
COX, C., 98*b*
CRESPO, G., 99*b*
CREW, L., 98*b*
CULLETON, B., 99*b*
CULTURAL EXPERIENCES: Reflection Points on, 16; responses to, 17*t*
CULTURAL HISTORICAL BACKGROUNDS: Reflection Points on, 11
CULTURALLY SENSITIVE TEACHING, 5, 50
CULTURAL MISCUES, 33–35, 49–50
CULTURAL OPENNESS, 25–32; Reflection Points on, 28
CULTURE: background knowledge on, 48; developing knowledge base about, 15–32; mismatch in, Reflection Points on, 5; resources on, 12*b*

CUMMINS, J., 4, 21–23
CUMMINS, N., 11
CURRICULUM: in Book Club *Plus,* 83–85

D

DAMPHOUSSE, K., 84*b*
DELACRE, L., 99*b*
DE LA LUZ REYES, M., 94
DELPIT, L., 12*b,* 94
DEWEY, J., 94
DIAZ-RICO, L., 26*b*
DILLER, D., 5
DISCUSSIONS: ELLs in, Reflection Points on, 43; Reflection Points on, 41; in small-group instruction, 55*t,* 60–66; speaking time in, 37–40, 38*t;* student and teacher participation in, 41–43

E

EDMONTON, F., 10–11
EISNER, E., 1, 5, 29, 50
ELLs. *See* English-language learners
EMPATHIC LISTENING, 31
ENGAGEMENT: and literacy learning, 73–75
ENGLISH-AS-A-SECOND-LANGUAGE (ESL) PROGRAMS, 24; resources on, 23*b*
ENGLISH-LANGUAGE LEARNERS (ELLs): context of work with, 1–14; in discussion, Reflection Points on, 43; innovative approaches to instruction of, 73*b;* instruction of, principles of, 90–94; knowledge base about, 15–32; new teachers of, resources for, 26*b;* opportunities for, 100–103; performance of, interpretations of, 17*t,* 18–19; perspectives on whole-group instruction, 43–51; reflections on, 67–78; small-group instruction with, 52–66; supporting comprehension for, Reflection Points on, 81; trends among, 1, 4; vocabulary instructional framework for, 88*t;* whole-group instruction with, 33–51
ERICKSON, F., 6
ESL PROGRAMS. *See* English-as-a-second-language programs
ETHNOGRAPHIC STANCE, 29, 95–96

F

FALTIS, C., 23*b*
FERDMAN, B.M., 95
FLORES DUEÑAS, L., 35

FLORIO-RUANE, S., 12*b,* 68, 81, 83, 84*b,* 103
FORD, M.P., 54*b*
FRANK, C., 5, 29–30
FREEMAN, D.E., 4, 26*b*
FREEMAN, Y.S., 4, 26*b*

G

GAMBRELL, L., 54*b*
GARCIA, E.E., 4
GARCIA, G.E., 73*b,* 87
GARLAND, S., 98*b*
GARRISON, J., 18
GAY, G., 5–6, 17, 30–31, 40, 50, 95
GEE, J.P., 31, 68, 71, 73–74, 84*b,* 94, 100
GEERTZ, C., 29
GEORGE, M., 68, 81, 83, 84*b*
GILL, J., 18
GOATLEY, V.J., 4, 8
GOUDVIS, A., 75*b*
GROUPING: by native language, 89–90
GUTIÉRREZ, K., 66, 93, 95

H

HABITS OF MIND, 94
HAKUTA, K., 4
HAMILTON, V., 98*b*
HAMILTON-MERRITT, J., 10
HARKLAU, L., 23*b*
HARRIS, V., 49*b*
HARVEY, S., 75*b*
HASTY, N.L., 81, 83, 84*b*
HIGHFIELD, K., 81, 83, 84*b,* 91
HILL, L., 49*b*
HISPANIC AMERICANS: children's books on, 99*b*
HMONG PEOPLE, 9–11
HOSOZAWA-NAGANO, E., 98*b*
HOWARD, G., 5, 96
HUDELSON, S., 23*b,* 68, 71
HUDSON-ROSS, S., 6*b*

I

IDENTITY: language and, 21
INITIATE-RESPOND-EVALUATE (I-R-E) PATTERN, 42, 68
INSTRUCTIONAL ANALYSIS, 67–78
INTERACTIONS: for ELL instruction, 92; Reflection Points on, 71; structuring, 71–75, 72*t*
INTERPRETATIONS: of ELL performance, 17*t,* 18–19; questioning, 29–30

INTERPRETERS, 33–35; and videotaped lessons, 2
I-R-E PATTERN. *See* Initiate-Respond-Evaluate pattern
IVEY, G., 87

J

JACOB, E., 30
JACOBS, J.S., 96
JANS, N., 26–27
JOHNSON, J.L., 49*b*
JONES, H., 99*b*
JORDAN, C., 30
JOURNAL WRITING, 55*t*
JUDGEMENT: suspension of, 29

K

KEHUS, M., 84*b*
KENNEDY, B., 12*b*
KNOWLEDGE: of culture and language, development of, 15–32; nature of, 18
KOTLOWITZ, A., 6*b*
KRASHEN, S.D., 21, 23*b*

L

LACAPA, M., 99*b*
LADSON-BILLINGS, G., 5
LANGER, J., 13
LANGUAGE: developing knowledge base about, 15–32; mismatch in, Reflection Points on, 5; resources on, 12*b*; and thought, 21
LANGUAGE ACQUISITION: factors affecting, 21–22; process of, 19–24; Reflection Points on, 19–20; resources on, 23*b*; support for, 24
LANKFORD, M.D., 99*b*
LATINOS/AS: children's books on, 99*b*
LAVE, J., 50, 77, 92
LEARNING: Reflection Points on, 35–36
LEARNING CENTER: and Book Club *Plus*, 85
LEE, M.G., 98*b*
LIFELONG LEARNING: teachers and, 96
LISTEN, D., 12*b*
LISTENING: empathic, 31; Reflection Points on, 30; resources on, 6*b*; to students, 2–6
LITERACY BLOCK, 83–85; format for, 87–88
LITERACY INSTRUCTION: Book Club *Plus* and, 79–103; cycle of, 86*t*
LITERACY LEARNING: ELLs and, 1–14
LITERACY MYTH, 100

LOTAN, R.A., 77
LOWRY, L., 79, 84–85

M

MACLACHLAN, P., 85
MAINSTREAM CLASSROOMS: resources for, 75*b*
MAJOR, E., 5, 26
MARINEZ, E.C., 99*b*
MARTINEZ, M., 54*b*
MASON, J.M., 77
MCCORMACK, R.L., 59
MCKAY, S.L., 23*b*
MCLAUGHLIN, M., 75*b*
MCMAHON, S., 4, 8
MCVEE, M.B., 35
MERCURI, S., 4
MICHIE, G., 6*b*
MIKE, J., 99*b*
MILLER CLEARY, L., 6*b*
MINAMI, M., 12*b*
MOHR, N., 99*b*
MONJO, F.N., 84
MOORE, D., 39
MORA, P., 99*b*
MORROW, L.M., 54*b*, 85
MOUA, DENG, 1–2; background of, 9–13; and language acquisition, 21–24; Valentine's booklet by, 2, 3*f*; on whole-group instruction, 43–51
MULTICULTURAL LITERATURE: resources on, 49*b*, 98*b*–99*b*

N

NATIONAL CENTER FOR EDUCATION STATISTICS, 30
NATIONAL CLEARINGHOUSE FOR ENGLISH LANGUAGE ACQUISITION & LANGUAGE INSTRUCTION EDUCATIONAL PROGRAMS, 4
NATIONAL COALITION OF ADVOCATES FOR STUDENTS, 4
NATIVE AMERICANS: children's books on, 99*b*
NATIVE LANGUAGE: in Book Club *Plus*, 79–81; grouping by, 89–90; Reflection Points on, 81
NEUMAN, S., 54*b*
NIETO, S., 5, 12*b*
NORTON, D.E., 49*b*

O

OAKS, E., 30
OBER, H., 99*b*

OPITZ, M., 54*b*
OPPORTUNITY: literacy and, 100–101
ORAL SUMMARY, 55*t*

P

PARATORE, J.R., 59
PARDO, L.S., 4, 8, 83, 84*b*, 91
PARKS, L., 39
PARKS, R., 98*b*
PATERSON, K., 20–21
PEARSON, P.D., 6
PEER GROUPS. *See* small-group instruction
PEREGOY, S.F., 73*b*
PHILIPS, S., 12*b*
PIERCE, B.N., 23*b*
POLACCO, P., 84
POYNOR, L., 68, 71
PRESSLEY, M., 54*b*
PRITCHARD, R., 26*b*
PROFESSIONAL ASSOCIATIONS, 96, 97*t*
PROFESSIONAL EDUCATORS: teachers as,
    94–98
PUNDIK, H., 84

R

RACISM: ELLs and, 48, 52, 61–62
RAPHAEL, T.E., 4, 8, 68, 81, 83, 84*b*, 91
RASINSKI, T.V., 75*b*
REED, G.J., 98*b*
REFLECTION POINTS: on cultural experi-
    ences, 16; on cultural historical back-
    grounds, 11; on cultural openness, 28;
    on discussion, 41; on ELLs in discus-
    sion, 43; on interactions, 71; on lan-
    guage acquisition, 19–20; on lan-
    guage/culture mismatch, 5; on
    learning, 35–36; on listening, 30; on
    small-group instruction, 53, 62–63;
    on small- versus large-group activities,
    70, 75–76; on speaking time, 37; on
    supporting ELLs' comprehension, 81;
    on teacher direction, 40; on teaching
    practices, 93
RICE, J., 99*b*
RODRIGUEZ, R., 21
ROGERS, T., 49*b*
ROSE, M., 30
ROSER, N., 54*b*
ROZENDAL, M., 73*b*

S

SAKAI, K., 98*b*
SCARLOSS, B.A., 77

SCHECTER, S.R., 4
SCHEU, J.A., 75*b*, 77
SCHOOLING CONDITIONS: and language ac-
    quisition, 22
SCHULTZ, K., 6*b*
SCHULTZ, S.E., 77
SHOJGREEN-DOWNER, A., 35
SHULTZ, J., 6
SIMON, D., 11
SIMONS, J., 23*b*
SIMS BISHOP, R., 49*b*
SMALL-GROUP INSTRUCTION, 54, 55*t*; charac-
    teristics of, 59–60; discussions in,
    55*t*, 60–66; with ELLs, 52–66;
    Reflection Points on, 53, 62–63; re-
    sources on, 54*b*; versus whole,
    Reflection Points on, 70, 75–76
SMITH, P., 12
SNEVE, V.D.H., 99*b*
SNOW, C., 19, 21
SOOK, N.C., 98*b*
SOTER, A., 49*b*
SPANGENBERG-URBSCHAT, K., 26*b*
SPEAKING TIME, 37–40, 38*t*; Reflection
    Points on, 37; in small-group instruc-
    tion, 52–53, 58–60, 60*t*
SPINDLER, G., 29–30
SPINDLER, L., 29–30
SPINELLI, J., 2, 15, 33, 52, 67, 101
STOWE, H., 98*b*
STRUCTURING: classroom activities, 69–71,
    70*t*; students' interactions, 71–75, 72*t*
STUDENTS: and discussions, 41–43; inter-
    actions of, structuring, 71–75, 72*t*;
    linguistic/cultural mismatches with
    teachers, 5; listening to, 2–6; percep-
    tions of learning experiences, 6
SWENTZELL, R., 99*b*

T

TAYLOR, D., 6*b*
TAYLOR, M., 98*b*
TEACHERS: and Book Club *Plus*, 82–83;
    and demographic change, 25–26; di-
    rection by, Reflection Points on, 40;
    and discussions, 41–43; and ELLs,
    39–40; as professional educators,
    94–98; resources for, 26*b*; and speak-
    ing time, 37, 38*t*; trends among, 4–5
TEACHING: resources on, 12*b*
TEACHING PRACTICES: and linguistic/cultural
    mismatches, 5–6; Reflection Points
    on, 93; in whole-group instruction,
    69*t*

TEXT SELECTION: for Book Club *Plus,* 85–86

THARP, R., 68

THEMATIC ORGANIZATION: in Book Club *Plus,* 90–92

THOMAS, W.P., 1, 19, 21–22, 24

TOMPKINS, G.E., 35, 75*b*

TSUCHIYA, Y., 91

TUNNELL, M.O., 96

TURCOTTE, M., 99*b*

U–V

UCHIDA, Y., 98*b*

VALDÈS, G., 95

VALENZUELA, A., 17, 40

VIDEOTAPING: of literacy lessons, 2

VOCABULARY: in Book Club *Plus,* 87–88; instructional framework for English-language learners (VISELL), 88*t*

W

WALKER-MOFFAT, W., 4, 10

WALTERS, A.L., 99*b*

WEED, K., 26*b*

WELLS, G., 68

WENGER, E., 92

WHEELER, B., 99*b*

WHOLE-GROUP INSTRUCTION: characteristics of, 36–37; with ELLs, 33–51; perspectives of ELLs on, 43–51; versus small, Reflection Points on, 70, 75–76; speakers in, 37–40, 38*t*; teaching practices in, 69*t*

WILLIS, A.I., 49*b*

WOLCOTT, H.F., 29

WOLFE, P., 68, 71

WOLLMAN-BANILLA, J.E., 49*b*

WONG, S.L., 23*b*

WONG FILLMORE, L., 19, 21

WORD STUDY: in Book Club *Plus,* 87–88

WORTHY, J., 87

Y–Z

YAMANE, L., 99*b*

ZEICHNER, K., 12*b*